Taste of
Puerto Rico

Angela Spenceley

Coconut Press, LLC

PUBLISHED BY POSTCARDS ETC, LLC

Copyright ©2017 by Angela Spenceley
Illustrations Copyright ©2017 Coconut Press, LLC
All rights reserved under International and Pan-American
Copyright Conventions. Published in China by
Postcards Etc, LLC

Library of Congress Control Number: 2008902472

Spenceley/Angela
Taste of Puerto Rico/by Angela Spenceley
ISBN: 1-901123-56-1

Manufactured in China

Published 2017

Contents

Endangered Puerto Rican Parrot

Introduction

It's hard to believe that it has been more than ten years since I wrote the first edition of *Taste of Puerto Rico* cookbook. I still remember photographing the food shots on my back porch with the warm, blue Caribbean Sea sparkling in the background, and my children trying to eat the props. Both kids are in college now, and fourteen cookbooks later, unfortunately, I have put on a few pounds. Yet, Puerto Rico remains unspoilt for the most part.

Despite the explosion of fast food restaurants on the island, in the last decade I have noticed a growing interest in traditional Puerto Rican cuisine, which spurred me to write the 380-page *Taste of Puerto Rico, Too.* Restaurants featuring rich, herb and spice-infused cooking flourish from Old San Juan to the shores of Rincon. On the mainland, the attraction for Puerto Rican cuisine increases steadily.

The recipes in this edition of *Taste of Puerto Rico* are my favorites, and for the most part, traditional. For those of you who haven't had a chance to visit Puerto Rico, I've included new photos of the island.

If you're new to Puerto Rican or tropical cooking, don't be afraid to substitute ingredients. That's how most Caribbean recipes came about—by improvisation. Explore the ethnic and produce section of your local grocery. You'll be surprised what ingredients you'll find.

Buen provecho!

Angela Spenceley

Angela Spenceley

El Morro Fortress, Old San Juan

Basic Facts About Puerto Rico

Geography

Puerto Rico is located in the eastern Caribbean, part of the Greater Antilles, a chain of islands that includes Cuba, Jamaica and Hispaniola. But at 35 miles long and 100 miles across, Puerto Rico is definitely the smallest of these islands at 18° north latitude, 66° west longitude. Including the offshore islands of Mona and Desecheo in the west, Culebra, Vieques and smaller cays to the east, Puerto Rico claims roughly 3500 square miles of land—about the size of the state of Deleware or the island of Corsica.

Puerto Rico is unique among Caribbean destinations because of its geographic diversity. Lush rainforests, bioluminescent bays, sunlit limestone caves compete with 750 miles of jagged coastline. The Cordillera Central (central corridor) of mountains bisects the island with rugged mountainsides dotted with pink impatiens flowers, coffee plantations and narrow and twisting roads. My sister and I were stuck on one of these steep passes in a tiny Toyota rental car and couldn't turn around! Not sure she has ever forgotten the incident either. In the northwest, Karst hills of exposed limestone rock flow across the landscape, and this is where you will find the caves. Flat coastal plains dominate the north and south allowing cultivation of citrus, sugarcane and pineapple. Virgin rainforests, such as the Caribbean National Forest (El Yunque) just an hour outside of San Juan, give way to remarkable dry, cactus forests to the south.

Climate

Puerto Rico averages a comfortable 82 degrees Fahrenheit year-round. Although, one night, while walking past the swimming pool at El San Juan Hotel, the temperature on the sign read 68 degrees —this was in December. And, yes, I wore a sweater.

Hurricanes do plague the Caribbean. But, thanks to steep mountain ranges, powerful storm winds are slowed before they do as much damage as they could to a flatter island.

Population

Puerto Rico, at 1,100 persons per mile, is one of the most densely populated areas in the world—a ratio higher than any of the 50 United States. There are 3.95 million people on the island, a third of which inhabit the greater San Juan area. More than 2 million Puerto Ricans have immigrated to the United States. Rumor has it, more Puerto Ricans live in New York City than in San Juan.

The people of Puerto Rico are a rich combination of European, Indian and African heritage. The first inhabitants were Taíno, Arawak and the fierce Carib Indians, originally from South America. Then came Christopher Columbus and the Spaniards, who killed the Indians either by slavery (mining silver and gold) or pestilence.

The next influx of immigrants occurred with the cultivation of sugarcane—African slaves, sold by Portuguese and Dutch traders in the early sixteenth century. In 1873, slavery was abolished, and by 1898, when Spain declared war on the United Sates, Puerto Rico became an American possession.

In order to understand the development of Puerto Rican cuisine, it is necessary to examine the time of Christopher Columbus a little closer.

History

The Spanish arrive ...

Things were pretty mellow on the island until Columbus landed in 1493. Taino Indians, migrated from South America, inhabited the island and called it *Borinquen* which means: 'land of the great lords.' The Tainos lived in small villages led by a *cacique* or chief. They were a simple, peaceful people with limited agricultural knowledge, subsisting on pineapple, cassava, yucca, arrowroot, peanuts, gourds, and peppers.

The women made bread from grated cassava, *casabe*, formed into loaves and baked on clay griddles. The bread kept for a long time in the hot climate. *Casabe* was an important part of the Taino diet.

Tobacco, corn, beans and squash were also cultivated. Living near the sea, diets were supplemented with seafood, turtles and an occasional parrot or iguana. A *pilon* was used to mash ingredients. Often meat or fish were tossed into what would later be known as a pepper pot, along with other liquids and vegetables, and simmered over an open fire for hours. This open air cooking method was called *barbocoa* (barbeque).

On April 17, 1492, Ferdinand and Isabella of Spain signed an agreement to finance Columbus's voyage to the Indies. The document declared that Columbus would become the viceroy and governor of all discovered land as well as 10% of the assets. On August 3, his fleet of three ships: the Nina, the Pinta, and the Santa Anna, discovered land on October 12. They landed at San Salvador

Island of Culebra, off Puerto Rico's east coast

in the Bahamas. Mistakingly thinking he had reached the East Indies, Columbus named the natives of the islands 'indians'.

His first voyage was so successful, Columbus had little trouble arranging for the financing of a second. This would not be an exploratory voyage, but rather a massive colonization effort. On September 25, 1493, Columbus left Spain with 17 ships and 1,500 men. Horses, sheep, cattle, pigs, seeds, citrus plants, wheat, barley, and the infamous sugar cane, traveled along. The Moors had taught the Spanish how to raise rice and pigeon peas, hence the favorite dish of 'arroz con gandules' or rice and beans was born in the new world.

On November 19, Columbus discovered Puerto Rico, inhabited by 50,000 Taino and Arawak Indians. The Indians would make the huge mistake of showing the Spaniards gold nuggets. Forced into mining, the Tainos were unable to farm, eventually dying from malnutrition and overwork.

In 1508 Ponce de Leon traveled from Santo Domingo to resume his search for gold. The Indians continued to die out from overwork, suicide, and murder. A number of the Spaniards married Indian women, but less than a 100 years later the Tainos were almost extinct.

Time passed, and the mild and fertile climate encouraged the raising of cattle, sugarcane, ginger, coffee and tobacco. Diets began to change as Spanish cooks incorporated their favorite ingredients, olives, bacalao (dried salt codfish), cilantro, sofrito, garlic, and other spices and herbs, with the local fare. Other foods native to Latin America were brought to the island with Spanish trade, such as cocoa from Mexico and yams from South America.

African culture and sugar cane production...

When the Spaniards discovered that little gold existed on Puerto Rico, they turned to other revenue-increasing methods in the mid-1500's. Sugar production. Every thing related to sugar production was imported: the technology, equipment, even African slaves.

The Africans brought okra, bananas, plantains, coconuts watermelon, black-eyed peas, tamarind and millet to the island. They taught the islanders basket, pottery making and their favorite way of cooking—frying.

Later, the Dutch, French, Italian and Chinese immigrants further influenced the culture and cooking to form *La Cocina Criolla*.

Rum industry...

Around this time, 17th century, an insatiable demand in Europe for sugar led to the establishment of hundreds of sugar cane plantations. Mills crushed the cane and extracted the juice, which was then boiled, causing crystallized chunks of sugar to form. The remaining liquid was melazas (from 'miel', the Spanish word for honey).

Molasses is a sticky syrup that still contains high amounts of sugar. Plantation owners soon noticed that the molasses mixed with water and left out in the sun would ferment. By the 1650's, this former waste product was being distilled into a spirit. Hence, the birth of the Caribbean rum industry.

Locally, rum was used as a panacea for many ills and pains afflicting those that lived in the tropics. Plantation owners also sold it at discounted prices, to naval ships to encourage their presence in local waters and afford protection from pirates. By the 1730's the British navy adopted the quaint custom of a daily ration of a half-pint of 160 proof rum. Later the rum was diluted by half with water and known as grog. This ration remained a staple in the British navy until 1969. And here I thought all this time grog was a version of light beer.

Grog aside, a thriving rum export trade developed, and rum was shipped to Great Britian and the British colonies in North America where it replaced gin. This export of rum to North America, in exchange for lumber and dried cod (still a culinary staple in the Caribbean and Puerto Rico) soon switched to the export of molasses to distilleries in New England. This was to circumvent a law from the British parliament, which protected British distillers by outlawing trade of rum directly between the colonies. Smuggling soon became rampant. Sounds a lot like money-laundering to me.

Shipment of molasses to manufacture rum in New England distilleries became part of the infamous 'slavery triangle.' This went hand in hand with the ever-increasing demand for slaves to run the sugar plantations. A skipper would leave with a cargo of rum to West Africa. There he would trade the rum for slaves and head back to the Caribbean to exchange the slaves for molasses. The molasses was transported back to New England to be distilled into rum.

The disruption of trade caused by the American Revolution and the rise of whiskey production in North America caused the slow decline of rum production. In Europe, the extraction of sugar from sugar beets lessened the demand for Caribbean sugar. Many plantations closed.

With the back scaling of the sugar industry, the population began to unify. Slaves, slave owners and Spaniards began to inter-marry. The Puerto Rican people became creole, bronze in skin tone, and more racially mixed than in other countries where slavery existed.

In the 18th and 19th centuries other agriculture: coffee, ginger, tobacco and cattle, flourished. Puerto Rican coffee was in demand in Europe. Ships from Spain, France, Portugal and England came to trade wine, cast-iron pots and utensils.

In 1865, Don Juan Serralles produced the first few casks of rum at the Hacienda Mercedita sugar plantation, near Ponce. This would later become the famous Don Q rum label. Don Q is the most popular rum in Puerto Rico.

Isla Verde and Condado, part of San Juan

Taste of Puerto Rico

In the 1930's Barcardi opened a distillery in Puerto Rico, now located in Catano, minutes from San Juan. Today, Puerto Rico is known all over the world for its light bodied golden rum, aged a minimum of three years.

Today...

Now, back to Puerto Rican cuisine or *comida criolla*. Today unfortunately, you can find a fast food chain restaurant on nearly every corner and these have had influence on island cuisine as well. Interestingly, some of the chains have adapted a pseudo Puerto Rican menu to their fare. It's not unusual to walk into a well-known steak house and see *alcapurrias* offered on the salad bar.

You will also find *come y vetes* (eat and run establishments) and other wonderful open-air eateries serving rice and beans, crab with rice, seafood pasteles. There are also many fine food restaurants, with eclectic menus: Thai-Latin, Mediterranean-Latin; even Chinese-Latin, offering expensive wines and candlelit ambiance. Old San Juan must have at least thirty fabulous restaurants. One could live in Puerto Rico and never dine at the same restaurant twice in one year.

Castillo Serralles in Ponce

What is
Puerto Rican food?

Almost all Caribbean cooking has been influenced by the Spanish, English, Danes, Africans, other Europeans and Orientals. Although Puerto Rican cooking bears a similarity to both Spanish and Mexican cuisine, what makes it different is the seasoning. Think of freshly cracked black pepper, *culantro* (wide coriander leaf), oregano, crushed rock salt, garlic, ginger, lime, sour orange and cinnamon. There is occasional use of hot peppers. However, most Puerto Ricans prefer small sweet peppers called *aji dulce*.

The island has a rich source of foods in its verdant hillsides. Traditional Puerto Rican recipes were born in these rural areas. Modern kitchens have replaced the old cooking methods to a greater extent with exception of a few utensils such as the mortar and pestle, a cast-iron cooking kettle similar to a Dutch oven.

The base of all Puerto Rican cuisine is *sofrito* and *achiote*. A caldero and a mortar and pestle are the indispensable tools behind it all.

Sofrito is made from: garlic; black peppercorns; rock salt; cilantro; *culantro*; parsley; oregano; sweet bell peppers; onions, and olive oil pounded into a fragrant paste, then sautéed with smoked ham, bacon, or chorizo, a Spanish sausage.

Achiote or annatto are the seeds of a small, flowering tropical tree in South America. The seeds are used to color and flavor oil.

A mortar and pestle mashes and melds garlic, onions, black peppercorns, rock salt, herbs and other spices into a heavenly seasoning paste.

A *caldero* is indispensibe for cooking rice recipes such as *arroz con pollo*. Made from iron (preferable) or heavy cast-aluminum, with a round bottom and straight sides, this kettle conducts heat evenly—a very important feature for Puerto Rican cooking.

Plátano, a.k.a. plantains are a mainstay in all the Caribbean islands. They're eaten ripe (my favorite) or green; served boiled, roasted or fried. The leaves of the plantain plant, as well as banana leaves, are used to wrap *pasteles.*

Soups are popular fare in Puerto Rico, either as a first course, or more often than not as a main meal such as *sopón de pollo con arróz* (chicken soup with rice) or *sopón de pescado* (fish soup). *Asopao* is a type of gumbo, much thicker than a soup, but not a casserole dish either, made with chicken or fish. *Asopao de pollo* is lovely with chicken, garlic, paprika, oregano, salt pork, ham, chili peppers, and tomatoes. *Sancocho* is perfect for the health conscious with its abundance of local vegetables, plantains and fresh meats.

At Christmas and other holidays, roasted pig is very popular. Basted with sour orange juice from *Seville* oranges and *achiote*, the roast is served with *aji-li-mojili*, a garlic sauce made with sweet peppers, vinegar, salt and olive oil.

Other popular types of main dishes include fried beefsteak with onions, rice with chicken, paella, and roasted meats served with a creole-style sauce.

While on a photo shoot in Puerto Rico, I discovered *tostones*, fried green plantain slices, lightly salted and crunchy.

Delicious *bacalaitos*, fried codfish fritters, can be found on every street corner, as well as *alcapurrias* (dumplings made from green bananas and *yautía*, stuffed with shellfish, chicken or fish), *pastelillos* (small flaky turnovers made from a flour dough, stuffed with cheese, meat, chicken, fish or guava paste) *frituras* (fritters made with bananas, vegetables, seafood, and meat) *piononos* (stuffed plantain rolls) pinchos (shish-kebabs) *empanadas* (deep-dish meat pot pies) and *surullos* (cornbread and cheese sticks).

Puerto Rican grown pineapple is among the sweetest and most fragrant in the world. Road side stands offer pineapple cut up and ready to eat. You'll also find *coco frio*. These are still green coconuts, chilled, tops cut off with a straw and spoon inserted in center to scoop out the jelly like meat and sweetly refreshing nectar. Papaya, mangoes, lime and tamarind are also grown locally and used to make iced fruit drinks.

Flan (custard) and *tembleque* (coconut custard) can be found on any good restaurant menu. The best flan I ever had was at the Hotel El Convento in Old San Juan, where it was served with a mango sauce. I've seen homemade *Cuadritos de Coco* (coconut squares) offered everywhere, even in gas station convenience stores. *Arroz con dulce* is made from cooked rice, coconut cream, sugar and cinnamon. Candied papaya, cooked in sugar and cinnamon, must be accompanied by *queso blanco* (white cheese).

Puerto Ricans love their coffee. Justifiably so, for centuries its reputation is the best in the world. Rumour has it the Pope will only drink Puerto Rican coffee, served very, very strong with hot, steamed milk.

Puerto Rican rums are the most popular worldwide. By law, they must be aged for years, hence their smoothness. Don Q rum is considered the best on the island.

So now you have a good idea of the diversity of *cocina criolla*. Puerto Rican cuisine embodies the spirit and the very best of Caribbean cooking.

Let's get started and learn about the unique tools and ingredients of Puerto Rican kitchens.

Luquillo Beach, near the Caribbean National Forest, an hour outside of San Juan

Glossary
of Ingredients

Adobo: Adobo is a blend of ingredients rubbed into fish, meat or poultry, excellent as a marinade, and a temporary preservative. I prefer to make a fresh batch when needed instead of using commercially packaged products with their accompanying preservatives.

Aji Dulce (Capsicum annuum): Sweet chili pepper, a dwarf with a mild and distinct flavor. Not to be confused with hot peppers.

Alcaparras: Capers. I prefer Spanish capers, but any variety of caper preserved in vinegar or oil will be fine. Taste them first. If too vinegary, soak in a bowl of cool water for 15 minutes, then rinse.

Annatto (Achiote): The use of *achiote* to flavor and color food has always been an important part of traditional island food. When combined with other herbs and spices, this emulsion gives Puerto Rican cuisine its distinctive aroma and flavor.

Annatto dates back to the Tainos who called it *bixa*. Lard or vegetable oil is heated in a saucepan at *low* heat, together with *achiote* seeds to release a rich, orange-yellow color and mildly pungent flavor.

The seeds are then strained and the emulsion reserved in a jar. Annatto's employ vary from flavoring and coloring rice dishes, adding an orange-brown color to white meats, substituting for tomatoes, and adding complexity to vegetable dishes. The use of this flavoring and coloring agent was the most efficient way to deal with the many staples not found in the kitchens of Spanish colonial Puerto Rico. Known as the poor man's saffron.

Breadfruit (pana, panapen): Large, roundish fruit (some as large as a soccer ball) of a tropical tree. A thick, greenish rind covers the sweet, starch flesh similar in taste to a potato. Do not eat raw. Fried green bread fruit are served as *tostones* to accompany drinks, meats, chicken or fish.

Cassava (yuca): Tuber of a shrub that has large palmate leaves. Can grow up to ten feet in height, native to Brazil and Mexico. Also known as manioc or yuca, not to be confused with yucca. Tuber is conical in shape, brown skinned, and the flesh can be white, yellow or red. Tubers can grow up to three feet in length and weigh 50 pounds or more. There are many varieties of cassava, all of which contain hydrocyanic acid, a poisonous substance eliminated by cooking or dehydration. Used to make tapioca.

Chayote (Christophene): Pear shaped, looks like a pale avocado, grows on a climbing plant extensively in the Caribbean. Similar in flavor to summer sqush.

Chironja: Cross between orange and grapefruit known only in Puerto Rico.

Chorizo: Highly seasoned Spanish pork sausage, sun-dried and hot to palate.

Cilantro: Coriander leaves.

Coconut (Coco): The use of coconut in Puerto Rican households is divided into two categories: *fresco de agua* (ripe with water) and *seco* (dry). The ripe with water coconuts are used in the making of desserts. The water is drained and used for making rum drinks, or simply as a refreshing, non-alcohilic beverage. The dry coconut is used to make coconut milk and intensely flavored sauces.

Codfish – dry and salted (bacalao): Dry, salted codfish has its origins in Europe, in the Scandinavian countries. It made its way with the Spanish explorers to Puerto Rico in the early sixteenth century. Inexpensive and popular in fritters and salads.

Criolla: Creole, a term used to describe Puerto Rican culture and cuisine.

Culantro (recao): Long, serrated leaves of a small herb, wide coriander leaf, which grows wild in the Caribbean.

Flan: Custard.

Gandul or gandules: Green pigeon peas.

Guayaba: Guava.

Garlic (Ajo): Spanish colonists introduced garlic to Puerto Rico.

Recently I had dinner at my friend Griselle's house. I watched her make a to-die-for shrimp and pasta dish. I couldn't believe how much garlic she added. Literally handfuls of the stuff (they sell crushed garlic in quart-size jars in Puerto Rican grocery stores). No wonder Griselle always looked so good, her skin clear, eyes bright. Garlic is an excellent detoxifier. However, later that evening when Griselle and I stopped by the Hotel El San Juan for after dinner drinks, no one came within two feet of us!

Ginger (Fengibre): A spicy root, ginger is the main ingredient in Island Bouquet Garni. Ginger is best when fresh. Purchase only as much as you will immediately need. Puerto Rican gingerroot is smaller and more pungent than the sort available stateside.

Green Onions (Cebollin): Also known as scallions, are used for their subtle flavor enhancement in sauces, salads, meat, fish and poultry. The high water content of scallions is beneficial when sautéing fresh herbs as it will provide some liquid to the drier ingredients. Garlic will cook and burn quickly upon a hot surface, but scallions will slow down the reaction time. Another use is to absorb some of the strong odors given off by lamb or seafood during cooking.

Ham (Jamon): Smoked cured ham is indispensable in the Puerto Rican kitchen. Used as a base for *sofrito*, and for soups, rice, main courses, etc. Fresh ham is used for pork fillings in *pastels*, *alcapurria* and *empanadas*.

Lechon: Cooked pig.

Machengo cheese: Originally from Spain, made with sheep's milk. A nice cross between white milk cheddar and a parmesan. Crumbly. Lovely piquant flavor, not too strong or too weak.

Mojo: Most popular sauce for seafood, features sweet cherry peppers and *culantro* leaf.

Olive Oil (Aceite de Oliva): Centuries ago, olive oil was highly prized in the New World and Puerto Rico, not just for cooking, but as a lamp oil, and lubricant for machinery. Because of piracy and foul weather, often it would be one or two years before a cargo ship reached the island. Prices on commodities and necessities soared, including olive oil.

Olives and Capers (Alcaparrado): *Alcaparrado* is a delicious combination of olives and capers preserved with vinegar and salt. Wonderful in *rellenos* as a stuffing, *pastels*, and salads.

Plantain (Amarillo): Fruit of the banana tree, a giant herbaceous plant native to Malaysia, related to the sweet banana. Also known as the 'cooking banana.' Ten to fifteen inches long, its green skin is thicker than that of the banana, its flesh firmer and not as sweet. When fully ripe, the skin turns black. Not to be eaten raw.

Recaíto: Seasoning made with recao, cilantro, onion, garlic and peppers that adds a distinctive flavor to food. Always part of the sofrito *base*.

Sofrito: Base for Puerto Rican cooking made from *recaíto* cooked with ham, tomato sauce and/or *achiote* (annatto)

Yautía: Starcy root (taro) of a tropical, large-leaved plant. Flesh is creamy white or yellow, similar in flavor and texture to Irish or Idaho potato.

Yuca: See cassava.

Stocking the Puerto Rican Pantry

Like every cuisine, Puerto Rican cooking has some basic ingredients. The backbone of this tropical cuisine lies in its seasonings and herbs.

Spices and herbs in order of importance:

- Black peppercorns (ground)
- Garlic
- Culantro
- Cilantro
- Oregano
- Parsley
- Ají Dulce (sweet chili pepper)
- Recao (herb used to impart piquant flavor)
- Onion and/or onion powder
- Annatto seeds
- Thyme
- Basil
- Bay Leaves
- Rosemary
- Sage
- Ginger
- Hot Chili Pepper
- Mustard
- Curry powder
- Cumin
- Allspice
- Cinnamon
- Anise
- Tarragon

Other important ingredients:

- Adobo
- Alcaparrado
- Bacalao (dry, salted codfish)
- Calabaza (West Indian pumpkin, substitute acorn or butternut squash)
- Coconut
- Gandules or Green Pigeon Peas (found dried or canned on mainland)
- Guanábana or soursop (find frozen concentrate in grocery)
- Habichuelas (beans, canned or dried)
- Ham, smoked (essential ingredient for sofrito and other dishes)
- Lechosa or papaya
- Parcha or passion fruit (frozen concentrate fine to use)
- Plátano or plantain (use green or ripe according to recipe)
- Recaíto
- Salchichas (Vienna sausages, a popular addition to rice dishes)
- Sofrito
- Tamarind (found in Latin groceries)
- Tocino, dry salt-cured pork (used in sofrito)
- Tomato sauce
- Vinegar

Tools and Techniques of Comida Criolla

M any of the items listed below are already in use in the modern kitchen. Some, like the *caldero*, a cast iron kettle, and the *pilon y maceta*, mortar and pestle, are new to non-Puerto Rican kitchens. Even so, they play an important part in the success of *comida criolla*.

Cast Iron Kettle (caldero): Cast iron kettles are indispensable because of their unique ability to absorb heat slowly and evenly. Made of heavy cast-iron (preferred) or cast-aluminum (now suspect as a link to Alzheimer's) with a round bottom and straight sides. A heavy kettle or Dutch oven may be substituted.

Cutting Boards: I prefer wood cutting boards over glass, which dulls a knife, or plastic, which can retain harmful bacteria. To sanitize wood cutting boards: using a fresh paper towel, dampen in warm water and add a $1/2$ teaspoon dish liquid or castile soap. Scrub board thoroughly, rinse and discard paper towel. Next, pour 3% hydrogen peroxide (available in drug stores) over all surfaces of cutting board and allow to sit for 20 minutes.

Rinse off with water, pat cutting board dry with fresh paper towels. Then pour white vinegar (I buy the $3.00 a gallon kind) over all surfaces of cutting board. Allow to sit overnight. No need to rinse. The vinegar will deodorize as well.

It's best to purchase four cutting boards: one for vegetables and herbs; one for meats; one for seafood; and another for kneading dough.

Food processor: Some people consider a food processor cheating, preferring to use a knife or mortar and pestle. But in this day of hustle and shrinking leisure time, a food processor makes quick work of tedious chores. Buy the best quality one you can afford.

The food processor has all but replaced the mortar and pestle.

Mortar and Pestle (Pilon y Maceta): The Tainos used a *pilon* carved from stone to grind their paints, root vegetables, grains and seeds. Early Spanish colonists also used the *pilon*. It was made from glazed clay, used to grind nuts and garlic and make *picada*, a seasoning base of garlic, saffron, paprika, parsley and lemon juice used in paella.

In Puerto Rico, the process of pounding and grinding spices and herbs in the *pilon* is called *machando* or *moliendo*.

Mortar and pestles can be purchased in metal, marble or wood, although I prefer the latter. Look for ones made or cedar, teak or oak. Eight to ten inches tall is a suitable size.

Curing: Combine 1/2 cup hot water with 1/2 cup white vinegar and pour into bottom of *pilon*. Allow to sit for one hour, then drain and dry with white paper towel. Add six peeled cloves of garlic, one at a time, and pound and grind into a smooth paste. To keep the garlic from flying out of the pilon, place one cupped hand over the rim of the mortar. Pound in an up and down fashion.

DO NOT WASH *pilon* AGAIN! Yes, that's right. Garlic is a marvelous disinfectant. Simply wipe out mortar after each use, cover with a brown paper bag, and store in cool, dry place. If you feel the need to clean it, before each use, pour 3% hydrogen peroxide into bottom of mortar, allow soaking for 20 minutes, drain and rinse, the wipe out with clean paper towel soaked in vinegar.

Uses: To mince, grind, crack or crush herbs, spices, grains. Excellent for making marinades or pastes.

Instructions: Place the largest pieces, i.e. garlic, onion, peppers, into the bottom first. Then the most textured, rock salt, peppercorns. Then, in one hand, take the pestle, place into center of mortar, cup your other hand over rim of mortar, then pound up and down slowly. Add liquid ingredients, olive oil, vinegar, etc. last. When a smooth paste has formed, cover with a clean dish towel and place in a warm spot to allow flavors to mingle. After removing paste, do not wash. You may wipe out with a cloth dampened in vinegar. A cured *pilon* adds a lovely complexity to a dish.

Chapter One

Basic Seasonings, Sauces, and Dips

The heart and soul of Puerto Rican cooking lies in its seasonings and marinades. The basic sauces are adobo, recaíto, sofrito, escabeche, ajilimójili, mojito de ajo and mojito isleño. Try the following recipes. They'll take a bit of time, but make extra and freeze in ice cube trays for future use in rice, fish, poultry and meat dishes.

Colorful local produce

Adobo

Quick and easy to make, the flavor difference between fresh and store-bought adobo is well worth the effort. This versatile seasoning is a blend of dry and wet ingredients rubbed into meat, poultry or seafood. Think of it as Puerto Rican *jerk* (similar to that of Jamaican jerk seasoning). Also may be used to season vegetables, rice, soups, oils, etc.

You will need your mortar and pestle for this seasoning. A food processor may be utilized, but at least grind the spices, especially the peppercorns, with the mortar and pestle first.

8 garlic cloves, peeled
1 1/2 teaspoons pulverized rock
   salt
1 teaspoon black peppercorns
1 teaspoon paprika
1/2 teaspoon ground cumin
1/2 teaspoon cayenne pepper
1 1/2 teaspoons fresh, chopped
   oregano
1 1/2 teaspoon fresh, chopped
   cilantro
1 teaspoon fresh, minced
   ginger
1/4 cup olive oil
3 tablespoons fresh lime juice
   or vinegar

1. Place garlic in bottom of mortar and pestle. Following the instructions in *Tools and Techniques* section, pound garlic into a paste. Add rock salt and peppercorns, pounding and incorporating into garlic paste.
2. Add paprika, cumin and cayenne, grinding into mixture.
3. Add oregano, cilantro and ginger. Pound until smooth.
4. Stir in olive oil and fresh lime juice.
5. Allow to sit for one hour. Use immediately or transfer to sterile glass jar and refrigerate. Use within one week or freeze for up to two months.

Yield: a little over a 1/2 cup

Recaíto

Recaíto is the base of most *sofrito* recipes. It's a little bit simpler and quicker to make than *sofrito*. You can use *recaíto* for all types of foods, and they needn't be Puerto Rican dishes. To make a larger batch and freeze, double or triple the recipe.

For the *culantro* used in these recipes, Anna brought me some seeds, which we grew while we worked on desserts.

$^1/_2$ cup coarsely chopped green
bell pepper
$^1/_2$ cup coarsely chopped yellow
onion
4 cloves garlic, peeled
2 teaspoons freshly chopped
culantro, also known as *recao*

1 teaspoon freshly chopped
cilantro
1 teaspoon freshly ground
peppercorns
$^1/_2$ teaspoon pulverized rock
salt

1. Place all ingredients in food processor. Process until mixture
   resembles oatmeal. Do not over-puree.
2. Place into a sterile jar and refrigerate for up to 3 days.
   Alternatively freeze for up to 2 months.

Yield: a little over 1 cup

Traditional Sofrito

*Transfer the sofrito to a sterile glass jar and refrigerate. Use within three
to four days. You can also freeze it in ice-cube trays and later transfer to a
plastic freezer bag.*

$^1/_4$ cup diced lean, cured ham
3 tablespoons salt pork
$^1/_4$ cup, plus 2 tablespoons
olive oil
6 garlic cloves, peeled and
crushed
$^1/_2$ cup chopped onion
$^1/_4$ cup chopped green bell
pepper
$^1/_4$ cup chopped sweet chili
pepper
1 tablespoon chopped fresh
culantro leaves

1 tablespoon fresh chopped
parsley
2 teaspoons fresh chopped
oregano (or 1 teaspoon dry)
1 teaspoon chopped fresh
cilantro leaves
1 teaspoon ground black
peppercorns
$^1/_2$ teaspoon pulverized rock
salt
$^1/_4$ cup, plus 3 tablespoons dry
sherry

1. Brown the cured ham and salt pork in a deep skillet over medium-
   high heat for 3 to 4 minutes until lightly browned on all sides.
2. Reduce heat to *low*, add olive oil, garlic and onion. Sauté for
   3 to 4 minutes until onion is just clear.
3. Add green bell pepper, sweet chili pepper, *culantro*, parsley,
   oregano, cilantro, salt and ground peppercorn. Sauté over about
   10 minutes, stirring occasionally.

4. Reduce heat even further and add sherry. Cover and simmer for $^{1}/_{2}$ hour. Remove from heat.

Yield: about 1 cup

Salsa de Escabeche

Escabeche sauce is popular throughout the island. Use white vinegar for a traditional recipe, or experiment with balsamic, raspberry and other exotic vinegars. Serve with fried fish, chicken, green bananas, or beans.

1 cup extra-virgin olive oil
2 medium yellow onions, sliced
$^{1}/_{2}$ cup white vinegar
1 teaspoon salt
1 teaspoon black peppercorns
2 bay leaves
3 large garlic cloves, peeled and
 minced

1. Heat the olive oil in a non-reactive 2-quart saucepan over moderate heat. Add onions and sauté for 5 minutes
2. Add all other ingredients, lower heat, and simmer for 15 minutes. Allow to cool completely.

Yield: about 2 cups

Hot habañero peppers

Annatto Oil (Achiote)

Nicely flavors rice dishes. Imparts a lovely pale yellow-red-orange shade. Used both as a coloring and flavoring in the islands.

4 tablespoons of annatto seeds   1 cup olive oil

1. Heat oil in small saucepan over low heat.
2. Add annatto seeds and cook until oil turns red-orange. Remove from heat at once. Do not overcook or this will lend a bitter flavor to oil.
3. Cool and strain. Discard seeds. Keep in refrigerator for up to 1 week.

Yield: 1 cup

Garlic and Pepper Sauce (Ajilimójili)

Traditionally served with barbequed suckling pig, this mildly pungent sauce goes well with poultry and seafood also. Note: you can prepare this recipe in a blender or food processor.

8 large cloves garlic, peeled $^1/_4$ cup white wine vinegar
1 $^1/_4$ cups chopped sweet chili $^1/_4$ cup fresh lime juice
   pepper
8 peppercorns
1 teaspoon pulverized rock salt
$^1/_2$ cup olive oil

1. Pound the garlic in a mortar and pestle until smooth. Add chili peppers, peppercorns and rock salt. Mash well.
2. Stir in olive oil, vinegar and lime juice.
3. Allow to sit one hour. Keeps for up to three days in the refrigerator.

Yield: a little more than 1 cup

Traditional Garlic Dipping Sauce
(Mojito de Ajo)

This habit-forming sauce is delicious alongside *tostones*, green bananas or other vegetable dishes. Try it on French Fries. Note: you may use a blender or food processor for this recipe.

8 large garlic cloves, peeled   1 teaspoon salt
1 cup extra-virgin olive oil

1. Pound the garlic cloves in a mortar and pestle. Drizzle in olive oil and salt.
2. Pour into a clean covered container in the refrigerator.

Yield: approximately 1 cup

Island Sauce (Mojo Isleño)

This is the island's most popular sauce to serve with fried fish or any other seafood. Featuring mild sweet cherry peppers and *culantro*, this sauce bursts with intense flavor. Keeps for several days in refrigator.

$^1/_2$ cup extra-virgin olive oil
1 cup minced yellow onion
6 large garlic cloves, peeled and crushed
1 *aji dulce* or Serrano pepper, seeded and minced
$^1/_3$ cup dry sherry
24 pimento-stuffed olives, chopped

2 tablespoons capers
$^1/_2$ cup canned tomato puree
$^1/_4$ cup fresh *culantro*
1 teaspoon fresh chopped oregano
1 teaspoon pulverized rock salt
1 tablespoon fresh lime juice
1 tablespoon vinegar

1. Heat olive oil in a skillet over medium heat. Add onion, garlic and peppers, sautéing until onions are clear. Deglaze pan with sherry.
2. Stir in olives, capers and tomato puree. Lower heat, add tomato puree and simmer for 5 minutes.
3. Fold in *culantro*, oregano, rock salt, lime juice and vinegar. Simmer, covered for 20 minutes.
4. If storing, transfer to reaction-proof container, glass or ceramic. Do not store in metal container.

Yield: a little over 2 cups

Taste of Puerto Rico

Mojito Sauce

Mojito goes well with just about everything. It can also rescue over-cooked fish or meat.

1/4 cup *sofrito*
1/2 cup ketchup
1 tablespoon minced *aji dulce* or other sweet cherry pepper

3 tablespoons dry Sherry or dry red wine
2 tablespoons fresh lime juice

1. Combine all ingredients in a small bowl. Allow to sit 30 minutes before serving with tostones and other finger foods.

Yield: just under 1 cup

Saffron Parsley Seasoning (Picada)

Picada is a seasoning paste whose key ingredient is saffron. Vibrant yellow and sultry, smoky in flavor.

1 teaspoon saffron threads
6 garlic cloves, peeled
1/2 teaspoon black peppercorns
1/2 teaspoon pulverized rock salt

1 tablespoon paprika
1/2 cup chopped Italian parsley
1 tablespoon fresh lime juice

1. Heat saffron in a small frying pan over moderate heat until crispy. Remove from heat and cool. Break up with your fingers. Set aside.
2. Grind garlic with a mortar and pestle until smooth. Add black peppercorns and rock salt; continue to pound with pestle.
3. Add paprika and saffron, breaking up saffron threads, and pulverizing. Add parsley and lime juice, processing into a smooth paste.
4. Keeps for 3 to 4 days in refrigerator. Really best if refrigerated overnight to allow flavors to mingle.

Yield: a little over 1/2 cup

Green Sauce (Salsa Verde)

Serve Salsa Verde with Arroz con Pollo, pork or beef. To use with fish, substitute fish stock for the chicken. This recipe makes around 4 cups and will keep for 2 days in the refrigerator. Since it doesn't freeze well, cut recipe in half if smaller amount is desired.

4 tablespoons butter
4 tablespoons flour
2 1/2 cups warm chicken broth
   (homemade is best, but
   canned is acceptable)
1/2 cup minced green bell
   pepper
1/2 small jalapeño pepper,
   seeded and minced
1 tablespoon freshly ground
   black pepper
3/4 cup finely chopped parsley
1/4 cup finely chopped cilantro

1. Melt butter in medium saucepan over low heat. Sprinkle in flour and stir with wooden spoon for 3 minutes until smooth to make a roux. Remove from heat.
2. Whisk in chicken broth until well combined.
3. Stir in bell pepper, jalapeño and black pepper. Return to low heat and simmer uncovered, stirring often, until thickened. Remove from heat.
4. Stir in parsley and cilantro. Serve at once.

Yield: about 4 cups

Rub for Pork Roast
(Aliño para Carne de Cerdo)

Use this paste on a fresh leg of pork or any other pork roast. Note: cut slits into the skin, and rub the meat with the paste, allowing to marinate overnight for peak flavor.

1/4 teaspoon salt
1 head garlic, peeled
1 tablespoon, plus 1 teaspoon
   freshly ground black pepper
1 teaspoon ground oregano
1/3 cup olive oil
2 tablespoon white wine
   vinegar
2 tablespoons fresh lemon juice

1. Place all ingredients in a food processor or blender. Process until smooth.
2. Refrigerate overnight to allow flavors to mingle.

Yield: enough rub for one 8- to 10-pound pork roast

Chapter Two

Appetizers
and Finger Foods

Cobblestone streets and historic buildings in Old San Juan

Basic Alcapurria Dough (Dumplings)

Alcapurrías are like stuffed dumplings, except the dough is made from green bananas and yautía (taro root) instead of flour. Yuca (cassava) may be substituted from the green bananas and yautía. Fillings vary from beef, chicken, and shellfish, which I am partial to. Alcapurrías may seem like a lot of work, but they are just so wonderful, it really is worth the effort. Wrap in aluminum foil, double bag in a plastic ziplock bag and freeze for up to three months.

1 quart water

2 teaspoons of pulverized rock salt

5 green bananas

2 pounds of *yautía* (taro root)

1 tablespoon achiote olive oil (annatto-colored, see *Basic Sauces, Marinades, etc.* chapter)

1 teaspoon vinegar

1. Fill a large bowl with 1 quart water and add salt. Peel bananas and taro root. Place into salt water. Allow to sit for 15 minutes.

2. Grate bananas and taro with the fine side of a hand grater. Or, cut vegetables into small pieces and process in food processor until smooth.

3. Mix banana/taro mixture with annatto-colored olive oil and vinegar. Transfer to glass bowl and cover with plastic wrap.

4. Refrigerate overnight or at least three hours.

Baking Instructions

1. Preheat oven to 375°F. Place a sheet of baking parchment on a sheet pan. Using an ice-cream scoop, place balls of dough, two inches apart, on the parchment.

2. Pressing down with the back of a teaspoon, make a $1/2$-inch deep indention in each alcapurria. Fill with 1 tablespoon of filling.

3. Press filling down with the back of a teaspoon and pinch the dough firmly shut over the filling.
4. Cover alcapurrias with aluminum foil and bake in preheated oven for 12 minutes. Ree foil, bake additional 12 to 15 minutes until alcapurrias are golden brown. Allow to cool for 5 minutes before removing from parchment paper.

Frying Instructions
1. For purists: try and use olive oil, it's more heart-healthy. Also a good quality deep-fryer will allow you to quickly fry alcapurrias. The less time spent in the fryer, the less oil will be absorbed. The key is to purchase a cooking thermometer and heat the oil hot enough so the alcapurrias will cook quickly. Heat 2 cups of olive oil to 375°F.
2. Cut off a large sheet of aluminum foil and baste lightly with olive oil. Place a scoop of the alcapurria dough on the foil. Depress center of dough with back of teaspoon and add a generous tablespoon of filling.
3. Press filling down with back of teaspoon, and pinch the dough firmly shut over the filling.
4. Using a spoon, gently glide the dough into the hot oil, being careful of splatters. Fry until golden. Drain on white paper towels.

Yield: enough for 16 alcapurrias

Beef Filling for Alcapurrias

This reminds me of beef turnovers (called patés) available at roadside stands in the U.S. Virgin Islands. Tantalizing flavor combination between the spices, olives and raisins.

$^1/_4$ cup olive oil
3 garlic cloves, peeled and minced
$^1/_4$ cup minced onion
2 teaspoons fresh chopped oregano
1 pound extra-lean ground beef
1 small habanero or other hot chili pepper, seeded and minced

$^1/_4$ cup chopped green bell pepper
3 tablespoons tomato paste
2 tablespoons apple-cider vinegar
$^1/_4$ cup raisins
10 pimento-stuffed green olives, chopped
2 tablespoons capers
$^1/_2$ teaspoon pulverized rock salt

1. Heat olive oil over medium heat in a large skillet. Add garlic, onion, oregano, ground beef and habanero pepper. Stirring continuously, brown beef on all sides.

2. Reduce heat and add green bell pepper, tomato paste, vinegar, raisins, olives, capers, and salt. Sauté for 8 minutes. Remove from heat and cool.

3. Fill alcapurrias with one generous tablespoon of filling.

Yield: enough for 8 alcapurrias

Chicken and Coconut Filling for Alcapurrias

Chicken thighs will produce a moister filling.

1/4 cup olive oil
3 garlic cloves, peeled and minced
1/4 cup minced yellow onion
1/2 small fiery chili pepper such as Serrano or Habanero, seeded and minced
1 teaspoon minced fresh ginger
1 pound boneless chicken breast or thighs, skin removed and chopped

2 teaspoons fresh chopped cilantro
1 tablespoon fresh lime juice
1/2 teaspoon pulverized rock salt
1/2 cup unsweetened coconut milk (canned is fine)
1/4 cup minced red bell pepper
1/4 cup minced green bell pepper

1. Heat olive oil in large skillet on low to medium heat. Add garlic, onion, chili pepper and fresh ginger. Sauté for 1 minute.

2. Add chicken and brown on all sides. Fold in cilantro, then lime juice, salt and coconut milk.

3. Add red and green bell peppers, continuing to cook over medium heat for 5 minutes.

4. Remove from heat and allow to cool.

5. Fill alcapurrias with one generous tablespoon of filling.

Yield: enough for 8 alcapurrias

Taste of Puerto Rico

Basic Pastelillo Dough
(Flaky Turnover)

This is the shortening version, light and flaky. Melts in your mouth. The healthier, olive oil version follows.

$3^1/_4$, plus 3 tablespoons of
  all-purpose flour
1 tablespoon salt
1 teaspoon baking powder
3 tablespoons, plus 2 teaspoon
  chilled vegetable shortening

1 egg, beaten
$^3/_4$ cup cold water
small amount of olive oil or any
  other vegetable (1 teaspoon
  is sufficient)
2 cups olive oil for frying

1. Sift flour, salt and baking powder into a large bowl. Using a fork or pastry cutter, cut shortening into flour. Mixture will be crumbly.
2. Whisk together egg and water in another small bowl.
3. Make a well in the center of the flour and add liquid. Stir at first with a fork, then grease your hands with oil, using your hands and fingers, knead dough until it forms a ball.
4. Transfer dough to floured cutting board, kneading for additional 5 to 7 minutes. Ball will be firm and smooth.
5. Divide dough into 12 pieces. Roll each piece individually with a rolling pin until the size of a small plate. For pastelillos to serve with drinks as appetizers, cut the pastry circles in $2^1/_2$ inch diameter.
6. Add a generous $1^1/_2$ to 2 tablespoons of stuffing to center; fold in half. Secure edges by pressing with a fork dampened with water.
7. Heat the 2 cups of olive oil to 375°. Using a spatula, pick up each pastelillo and gently slide into oil, mindful of splatters. Fry until golden; draining on white paper towels.

Yield: 12 pastelillos, or 24 of the appetizer size

Surfers in Rincon

Pastelillos (Meat Turnovers)

Pastelillos are small, flaky turnovers made from a flour dough, filled with seasoned ground beef, chicken, pork, seafood, cheese or guava paste. I love these. No wonder I had to spend two hours a day at the gym while working on this book. Baking, instead of frying (both techniques explained) helps with the waistline issue a bit. Because they are usually fried, pastelillos come under the catergory of frituras (frita means fried). The term fritura includes all fried finger foods. Frituras are to Puerto Rico what the paté is to the Virgin Island West Indian, the egg roll to the Chinese, the taco to the Mexican and the calzone to the Italian. Not to be confused with pasteles (made from a root vegetable dough, usually filled with pork, wrapped in banana leaves and boiled).

Saffron Crab Filling for Pastelillos

Substitute chopped shrimp or lobster for crab. For a rich, beef filling, see Beef Filling for Alcapurrias; pork, see Traditional Pork Filling for Pasteles.

2 tablespoons olive oil

1 teaspoon annatto-colored olive oil

1/4 cup diced green bell pepper

1 sweet chili pepper, diced and seeded

3 cloves garlic, crushed

1/2 cup yellow onion, minced

1 teaspoon saffron threads

1 tablespoon chopped canned pimento

1 tablespoon capers

8 pimento-stuffed olives, chopped

1 teaspoon freshly cracked black pepper

1 teaspoon salt

1 pound crab meat, fresh or canned, shredded and cartilage pieces removed

1. In a deep skillet or medium saucepan, heat the olive oil and annatto-colored oil over medium heat. Sauté the green pepper, chili pepper, garlic and onion for 2 minutes until soft. Add saffron, pimento, capers, olives, pepper and salt, cooking additional 5 minutes.

2. Fold in crab, reduce heat and simmer for 10 minutes. Remove from heat and allow to cool before filling pastelillos.

3. Use 1 1/2 to 2 tablespoons filling for each pastelillo. Follow instructions instructions in basic pastelillo dough for sealing turnover, baking or frying.

Yield: enough for 12 pastelillos, or 24 appetizers

Basic Pastele Dough and Assembly

Be sure to place vegetables in large pot of cold, salted water after peeling to keep them from turning black:

Dough:

- 5 green bananas, peeled and grated
- 2 large green plantains, peeled and grated
- 1 pound peeled and grated yuca (cassava), use frozen one if possible, it's more convenient
- 1 pound yautía (taro), peeled and grated
- 1 pound calabazo (West Indian pumpkin), peeled and diced, substitute butternut squash if needed
- 1 pound white yautía (taro) or Idaho potataoes, peeled and diced

- 1 cup pork stock
- 6 tablespoons annatto-colored olive oil
- $1/3$ cup milk
- 1 tablespoon salt

Wrapping:

- 12 banana leaves
- 12 sheets cooking parchment
- $1/3$ cup annatto-colored olive oil
- kitchen twine
- 2 teaspoons salt
- water to boil pasteles
- raffia (optional)

1. Fit food processor with grated blade. Have a large bowl handy to hold grated vegetables.

2. Drain water from vegetables. Process small amounts of the vegetables at a time. Add a little pork stock until the vegetables have the consistency of oatmeal. Once all the vegetables are pureed, place in large bowl.

3. Stir in any remaining pork stock, 6 tablespoons annatto oil, and the $1/3$ cup milk. Use your hands to mix and remove any large chunks of vegetables. Batter should have a smooth silky surface.

Assembling of pasteles:

1. Wash and dry banana leaves. Trim to 8 by 8 inches with kitchen shears. Fill a deep baking dish with hot water and dip leaf in water until it wilts. Remove and place on a clean kitchen towel. Pat dry. Repeat process with all leaves.

2. Cut kitchen twine into 12, 30-inch pieces and set aside.

3. Set up an assembly area as follows: parchment paper; banana leaves; grated vegetable dough; pork filling and twine.

3. Place 1 sheet of parchment on a wood cutting board. Lay a banana leaf on top of the parchment. Spread 1 tablespoon of annatto oil over the leaf surface. Spoon $1/2$ cup of the dough in the middle of the leaf. Smooth the dough with the flat side of a spoon to a 5 by 5-inch square.

4. Next spoon a generous $1/4$ cup of pork filling over the dough area.

5. To fold pastele: Grip the parchment and banana leaf together by the lower corners. Fold in half (away from your body) so that the filling is completely covered by the dough. Fold the ends in toward the middle. Fold in half in twice more. You should have a rectangle about 3 inches wide.

6. Tie pasteles in pairs with folded sides inside. Tie securely with twine.

7. Fill a large kettle or stockpot with water and bring to a boil. Add 2 teaspoons salt. Lower pasteles and bring back to a boil. Reduce heat and simmer for 45 minutes to 1 hour. Turn once during cooking period.

8. Remove from boiling water and drain. Open parchment paper and slide banana leaf rectangle onto plate. At this point, you may decoratively re-tie the pasteles with raffia (straw cord). Serve warm as a snack or main course.

Yield: 12 pasteles

Pasteles (Steamed Meat Patties)

Pasteles are a part of being Puerto Rican. Not having pasteles at Christmastime is like not having gifts under the tree. Pasteles differ from pastllillos in that they are boiled in plantain leaves and not fried. The dough is made from grated root and other vegetables. Pork is the traditional filling, but seafood and chicken may also be used.

Traditional Pork Filling for Pasteles

1 pound boneless pork roast, diced in $1/2$-inch pieces
2 tablespoons adobo
2 tablespoons annatto-colored oil
$1/2$ cup smoked ham, diced finely

1 cup recaíto
1 cup of tomato sauce
$1/2$ cup cooked chickpeas
$1/2$ cup raisins
2 tablespoons shredded, unsweetened coconut

1. Follow instructions for pasteles dough in previous recipe. Season pork with adobo. Heat annatto-colored oil in skillet and sauté the pork and ham over medium heat for 5 minutes until lightly browned on all sides.
2. Add recaito and reduce heat. Simmer for 3 minutes, then stir in tomato sauce, cooking additional 20 minutes. Pork should be cooked through. Fold in chickpeas, raisins and coconut. Heat through. Remove from stove and set aside.
3. Follow assembly instructions for pasteles.

Tostones (Plantain Chips)

Tostones are diagonal slices of green plantain, partially fried, then flattened and fried again, until golden. The texture is crisp on the outside, creamy on the inside. Tostones are to Puerto Ricans what French fries are to Americans. Not to be confused with bagged plantain chips. Serve by themselves with cocktails, or an accompaniment to meat and fish dishes.

1 large green plantain, peeled,
  and cut into diagonal slices
  1/2-inch thick
3 quarts water
2 cloves garlic, crushed
  (optional)

1 tablespoon pulverized rock
  salt
vegetable oil for frying

1. Soak plantain slices for 30 minutes in the salted water and garlic.
   Remove from water and pat dry with paper towels.
2. Heat 3 tablespoons of oil in deep skillet or frying pan. Sauté until
   soft, but do not allow to become crunchy on ouside. Remove from
   hot oil with tongs, and drain on white paper towels.
3. Place a sheet of waxed or parchment paper over plantain slices and
   flatten. Dip into salted water and fry again until golden on all sides.
4. Drain on paper towels and salt to taste. Serve with Mojito Sauce

Yield: 12 to 15 tostones

Chicken Asopao with Plantain Balls

*Chickens run wild all over the island. Perhaps that is why there are so
many versions of chicken soups—the over abundance of the birds.*

2 cups uncooked rice
2 cups water
1 3-pound chicken cut into
  pieces
1/4 cup adobo
1 bay leaf
1 green plantain, peeled
1 tablespoon all-purpose flour
3 tablespoons olive oil
1/4 cup minced yellow onion

4 cloves garlic, crushed
1/4 cup dry Sherry
1 cup diced ripe tomato
6 cups chicken stock
1 cup fresh sweet peas
2 tablespoons fresh chopped
  cilantro or culantro
1 red bell pepper, roasted, skins
  removed and diced

1. Rub the chicken pieces with adobo and allow to marinate in the
   refrigerator for a couple hours.
2. Soak the rice in the 2 cups water for 1 hour.
3. Place 4 cups of water in deep kettle or stock pot. Heat to boiling
   and add chicken and bay leaf. Reduce heat, cover and simmer for
   20 minutes. Remove from heat. Bones and skin may be removed
   from chicken. Cut chicken into bite-size pieces. Set aside.

4. Grate green plantain into shreds. Place a spoonful in palm of hand, add a pinch of flour and form into a ball. Set aside.

5. Heat olive oil in a skillet. Sauté onion and garlic. Deglaze pan with Sherry.

6. Drain rice, pour into kettle with chicken stock. Add chicken and onion/garlic/Sherry mixture. Add plantain balls. Bring to a boil, reduce heat and simmer for 13 minutes.

7. Add tomatoes and fresh peas. Simmer for additional 7 minutes. Stir in cilantro. Ladle into soup bowls, topping with roasted peppers. Serve hot with tostones and chilled beer.

Yield: serves 6

Shellfish Stew (Asopao de Mariscos)

If you like seafood, the fragrance of this shellfish stew is heady. Use the freshest ingredients possible and don't stint on the garlic. The extra time needed to prepare this stew is worth it.

2 cups long-grain rice
2 cups of water
1 1/2 cups sofrito
6 cups chicken stock
1 lobster tail (1 pound), cut in pieces
1/2 pound raw crabmeat, cartilage removed and flaked
1/2 pound shrimp, raw, shelled, and deveined

1/2 pound mussels, scrubbed, beards scraped away; or 3/4 cup canned
1 cup fresh sweet peas, uncooked
2 tablespoons capers
8 pimento-stuffed olives
1/2 cup dry Sherry
2 pimentos cut in strips

1. Soak rice in the 2 cups of water for 1 hour.

2. Heat sofrito in deep kettle or caldero over medium heat for 3 minutes. Drain rice and add to kettle. Add chicken stock and bring to boil. Reduce heat and simmer for 10 minutes.

3. Fold in lobster and cook additional 3 minutes. Return to a boil, add shrimp, crab, mussels and peas. Cook 3 minutes. Remove from heat.

Stir in olives and capers. Add sherry. Allow to sit for 10 minutes before serving. Garnish with pimento strips.

Yield: serves 6

Yokahu Tower in the Caribbean National Forest, El Yunque

Chapter Three

Soups

Beef Stew (Sancocho)

Sancocho, also known as Ajiaco Criolla (chili based stew) is usually served on special occasions. The preparation time is long, and the ingredient list is even longer. Enjoy this time in the kitchen with friends, an ice-cold beer or a refreshing libation made with smooth Puerto Rican rum.

3 tablespoons olive oil
6 garlic cloves
2 1/2 pounds beef chuck, trimmed and cut into 1 1/2 inch cubes
1/4 pound smoked ham diced
1/2 cup minced onions
1/2 cup diced green bell pepper
1/4 cup minced celery
1 *aji ducle* (sweet cherry pepper) seeded and diced
1 cup sofrito
1 cup tomato sauce
1 1/2 cup diced ripe tomatoes
4 quarts beef stock
2 yellow plantains, peeled and sliced in 1-inch wheels
1/2 cup diced pumpkin (West Indian pumpkin or any other dry pumpkin or squash such as butternut)

1 cup peeled and diced yam
1 cup peeled and diced yautía (taro root)
1 cup peeled and diced cassava root
1 cup diced and peeled new potatoes
3 ears fresh corn, peeled and cut in 1-inch pieces
1 large chayote, peeled, cored and cubed in 1-inch pieces
1 tablespoon salt
1 tablespoon freshly ground pepper

1. Heat olive oil in a deep kettle (caldero), cast iron pot or heavy stockpot over medium heat.
2. Add garlic, beef, ham and onions. Stir and brown beef and ham on all sides. Fold in pepper, celery, sweet chili pepper and sofrito. Reduce heat and simmer for 5 minutes.
3. Add tomato sauce, tomatoes and 4 cups of the beef stock. Cook uncovered until liquid is reduced by half.
4. Add remaining stock, plantains, pumpkin, yam, yautía, cassava, potatoes, corn, chayote, salt and pepper. Cook another 30 minutes until meat and vegetables are tender. Serve with a crisp green salad and Puertorican beer such as Medalla.

Yield: serves 6

Black Bean Soup with Shrimp
(Frijoles Negros con Camarones)

A sale on shrimp at the market resulted in the birth of this recipe. The addition of shellfish makes this soup a complete protein. Serve at lunch with hot rice and crusty bread, or as a first course at dinner.

5 ounces black beans, rinsed
   and picked over for stones
   and soaked overnight
2 1$^{1}/_{2}$ cups water
$^{1}/_{2}$ teaspoon ground cumin
$^{1}/_{2}$ teaspoon dried oregano
1 bay leaf
4 tablespoons annatto oil

2 cloves garlic, crushed
$^{3}/_{4}$ cup minced onion
2 medium tomatoes, chopped
2 cups chicken stock
1 pound cooked shrimp, tails
   removed, but left whole
$^{1}/_{4}$ cup dry sherry

1. Combine black beans, water, cumin, oregano,and bay leaf in a medium soup pot. Bring to boil over medium-high heat, reduce heat, cover and simmer for one hour. Remove from heat, take off cover and allow to cool for 30 minutes, stirring occasionally

2. Remove bay leaf and puree in food processor, one cup at a time.

3. Heat annatto oil in large skillet and sauté garlic and onion until just soft, but not browned. Add tomato and cook for another minute.

4. Add garlic mixture to food processor and puree. Add chicken stock, return to soup pot and bring to simmer. Fold in cooked shrimp and heat through another ten minutes.

5. Remove from heat and allow to sit for 15 minutes, covered. Stir in sherry and ladle into soup bowls.

Yield: 4 servings

Seasoned Rice

You may substitute olive oil for the bacon or salt pork rind.

1 slice bacon or 1$^{1}/_{2}$-inch cube
   of salt pork rind
$^{1}/_{3}$ cup sofrito
1 tablespoon annatto-colored
   olive oil

2 cups long-grain white rice
$^{1}/_{2}$ teaspoon salt
4 cups cold water

1. Fry the bacon or salt pork rind in a kettle over medium heat until crispy. Remove meat. Crumble bacon and set aside Add sofrito and annatto oil and sauté for 5 minutes over moderate heat.

2. Stir in rice and salt, mixing well. Immediately pour in cold water and stir, scraping bottom of pot.
3. Bring to a rapid boil, then reduce heat to medium. Cook uncovered until water cooks down and top of rice is bubbly.
4. Reduce heat to low and cover. Cook for 20 minutes.
5. Uncover, flip rice over with a fork from the bottom up. Cook for additional 5 to 8 minutes until all water is absorbed.

Yield: serves 6

Yellow Rice

Don't use an instant or Uncle Ben's type of rice with this recipe. It won't work.

4 tablespoons annatto-colored olive oil
2^1/$_2$ cups medium grain rice
2 chicken bouillon cubes, crushed

1 tablespoon sofrito
3^1/$_2$ cups water
2 teaspoons salt

1. Heat the olive oil in a medium saucepan over moderate heat. Sauté the rice for 2 minutes until glistening.
2. Add chicken boullion and stir well until cubes are dissolved.
3. Stir in sofrito and cook for 1 minute.
4. Add water and salt and bring to boil over high heat.
5. Reduce heat once water has nearly evaporated. Stir a couple times and cover.
6. Simmer for 25 minutes until rice is tender.

Yield: 4 to 6 servings

Pigeon Peas and Rice
(Arroz con Gandules)

Christmas in Puerto Rico would not be the same without arroz con gandules.

3 slices bacon or 4 tablespoons vegetable oil (add 1 teaspoon salt if using oil instead of bacon)
1/2 cup sofrito
1 tablespoon alcaparrado

2 cups long-grain rice
4 cups cold water
1/2 cup diced lean smoked ham
1 1/2 cups shelled pigeon peas
2 tablespoons tomato sauce

1. Fry the bacon or heat the oil in a kettle over medium heat. When bacon is crisp, remove, crumble and set aside.
2. Sauté the sofrito for 5 minutes. Add alcaparrado and rice. Immediately add water and stir.
3. Add ham, pigeon peas and tomato sauce. Return bacon to kettle. Stir well to mix.
4. Bring to a boil, then reduce heat to medium. Cook uncovered until water boils down and top of rice looks bubbly.
5. Reduce heat to low, cover and cook for 25 minutes.
6. Remove cover, fluff rice once with a fork from the bottom up. Cook for additional 8 to 10 minutes until all water is absorbed. Serve with roast pork, turkey or ropa viejo.

Yield: serves 6 to 8

Chapter Four

Rice and
Bean Dishes

Rice and Beans (Arroz con Gandules)

Every Caribbean island has a technique for rice and beans. But the best tasting recipes come from Puerto Rico. I think it's the cilantro that makes the difference.

3/4 cup sofrito
1 can tomato sauce
2 tablespoons, plus 1 teaspoon
  alcaparrado
4 tablespoons annatto-colored
  oil

2 cups long grain rice
3 cups hot water
1 16-ounce can pigeon peas
salt and pepper to taste

1. Sauté sofrito, tomato sauce, alcappardo in the annatto-colored oil in a heavy stockpot or kettle over moderate heat for 5 minutes.
2. Add rice and hot water and cook uncovered, bringing to a boil until most of the water has been absorbed.
3. Once water has been absorbed, fold in pigeon peas, stirring gently a couple times from top to bottom. Do not stir after this point or the rice will go gummy or amogollao.
4. Cover and reduce heat to low. Simmer for 25 minutes. Season to taste with salt and pepper.

Yield: 8 servings

Rice with Crab (Arroz Con Jueyes)

Great land crabs exist all over the Caribbean. I'll never forget the time I was on a photo shoot on Grand Cayman, about a mile from where they filmed the movie The FirmXXX. There were literally thousands of crabs crossing the roads. Our jeep couldn't move, so I jumped out to shoo them away. I felt so bad. All these cars were running them over. Eventually I gave up and we had no choice but to drive over the poor creatures to get to where we were going. Our island hostess later explained that the extraordinary crab sighting meant a hurricane later in the season. Later that year, Hurricane Marilyn struck.

Note: Lobster or shrimp may be substituted for the crab.

4 tablespoons extra-virgin olive oil
1 tablespoon annatto oil
1/4 cup diced cured ham
1/2 cup sofrito
2 green frying peppers, seeded and chopped
1/2 teaspoon dried oregano
1/2 teaspoon dried basil
3 tablespoons alcaparrado
2 tablespoons tomato paste
1/4 cup 2 tablespoons dry white wine
3 1/2 cups water
1 cup chicken broth
3 cups long-grain rice, rinsed
2 1/2 cups cooked crabmeat
salt and pepper to taste

1. Brown the ham in a deep kettle in the annatto oil and olive oil over medium heat. Stir in sofrito and frying peppers. Sauté for 5 minutes until peppers are just soft.

2. Fold in oregano, basil, alcaparrado and tomato paste, cooking 2 more minutes.

3. Pour in white wine, water and chicken broth. Turn heat on high and bring to boil. Add rice and stir. Reduce heat to medium, and cook uncovered until water reaches level of rice.

4. Fork over rice from top to bottom. Reduce heat to low, and cover uncooked for 10 minutes.

5. Fold in crabmeat, forking over rice again. Cover and cook over low heat for 20 minutes. Season to taste with salt and pepper.

Yield: 6 servings

Land crab frequently found in the Caribbean islands.

Traditional Puerto Rican Paella

Spain's famous paella dish originated in the seaside port of Valencia. Along with many other culinary gifts from the Spaniards, paella made its way across the ocean to Puerto Rico. Annatto oil adds a beautiful pale orange color and smoky flavor.

2 pounds chicken pieces, rinsed and patted dry
2 teaspoons salt
1/2 pound lean pork, diced
1/4 cup olive oil, divided
3 tablespoons annatto oil
1 cup minced yellow onion
2 green frying peppers, seeded and diced
6 large cloves garlic, minced
2 chorizos, cut in 1/2-inch pieces
2 tomatoes, peeled, seeded and diced
1/2 teaspoon saffron threads
2 cups long-grain rice

4 1/2 cups chicken or fish stock
1 teaspoon freshly cracked pepper
2 pounds frozen raw shrimp
1 pound frozen raw lobster meat, shells removed and coarsely chopped
1 10-ounce can clams, drained
1 cup frozen or fresh green peas
1 seven-ounce can pimentos
1 bunch fresh asparagus, trimmed and cooked (you may use canned)
12 to 18 frozen mussels, ready to cook

1. Season chicken and pork with salt. Heat 1/4 cup of the olive oil in a deep kettle or skillet. Brown chicken and pork on all sides over medium heat. Remove from skillet and reserve.
2. Preheat oven to 350°F. Drain olive oil from skillet and discard.
3. Add remaining 1/4 olive oil to skillet along with annatto oil. Reduce heat slightly and sauté onions, peppers and garlic for five minutes.
4. Stir in chorizo and tomatoes. Remove from heat while crisping saffron.
4. In a small frying pan, dry heat saffron over moderate heat until crunchy. Remove from heat and cool. Crumble with hands into onion/pepper mixture and return to stove over moderate heat.
5. Add rice and 3/4 cup of stock, along with cracked pepper. Cook for 5 to 6 minutes, stirring often. Add remaining stock, stirring well.
6. Transfer to oven-proof casserole or paellera (special paella dish)
7. Arrange chicken, pork, shrimp, lobster, clams and peas, so that they are covered by stock. Cook for 45 minutes until all liquid has been absorbed.

8. Follow cooking instructions on package of mussels. If the paella has come out a bit dry, pour some of the seasoned liquid from the cooked mussels over the rice.

9. Garnish with cooked asparagus strips. Arrange mussels over top.

Yield: serves 6

Pegao

The golden brown, crunchy rice that adheres to the bottom of a pot is called pegao. A favorite of Puerto Ricans, there's a true art to making it. I burnt the pegao several times before I became successful at it. Use extra oil and cook the rice, uncovered, for an extra 10 to 15 minutes. Keep in mind if you want a lot of pegao, you'll want a pot with a larger bottom, i.e. more pegao.

Puerto Rican Stewed Beans
(Habichuelas or Guisantes Guisados)

1 pound dried beans, soaked
1 tablespoon annatto oil
1 ounce salt pork, diced
1/4 cup diced cured ham
1 large sweet chili pepper, seeded and minced
1/2 cup sofrito
1 1/2 tablespoons tomato paste
2 tablespoons dry sherry

1/2 teaspoon dried oregano
1/2 medium ripe plantain, peeled and cut in 1 inch slices
1/2 cup water
1/2 pound pumpkin, peeled, seeded, cubed and boiled until tender

1. Place the dried beans in a 5 quart saucepan. Cover 3 times bean volume with water. Bring to boil, uncovered. Reduce heat to simmer and continue to cook uncovered until tender. Test for doneness at 45 minute mark.

2. In a large skillet or frying pan, heat annatto and olive oil. Brown salt pork and ham on all sides.

3. Stir in pepper and sauté for 2 minutes. Fold in sofrito, tomato paste, sherry and oregano. Cook for additional 1 minute.

4. Stir sofrito mixture into bean pot. Add plantain and 1/2 cup water. Cover and simmer for 10 minutes.

5. Mash pumpkin and add to bean pot. Stir and cook, covered for another 10 minutes.

Yield: 8 to 10 servings

Tip – Rice

* To reheat cooked rice, place rice in an appropriately sized saucepan. Add 2 tablespoons water per cup of cooked rice. Cover and simmer over low heat until hot and all water is absorbed.
* To keep rice warm, place two layers of white paper towels under the lid. This will absorb steam and keep rice from becoming gooey.
* To cook a large amount of rice, use a pot with a large bottom, at least 10 inches in diameter.

Puerto Rican Black Beans
(Frijoles Negros)

This is often served as a side dish in Puerto Rico. Make an entire meal by filling bowls with hot white rice and top generously with beans, garnish with minced onions.

1 pound soaked black beans
  (see above for tips)
1/4 cup olive oil
1/2 cup minced yellow onion
1 green frying pepper, seeded
  and minced
3 sweet chili peppers, seeded
  and minced
4 large cloves garlic, crushed
1 bay leaf

1/2 teaspoon dried oregano
1 1/2 teaspoons salt
1/2 teaspoon cumin
1/2 teaspoon sugar
1/2 teaspoon cracked black
  pepper
1/2 cup water
1/4 cup white wine
1 tablespoon vinegar
1/2 cup minced raw onion

1. Place soaked beans in a 5-quart saucepan. Cover with 3 times their volume with water. Bring to boil, uncovered. Reduce heat and simmer for 45 minutes. Do not boil as it will break their skins. Add water as needed. Test for doneness by rubbing a couple beans between your fingers to see if they will mash.

2. Heat olive oil in a heavy skillet. Sauté onions, peppers and garlic over moderate heat until onion is tender, about 5 minutes.

3. Add 1 cup of cooked beans and mash.

4. Add bay leaf, oregano, salt, cumin, sugar and black pepper. Stir and fold in remaining beans, water and wine.

5. Cover, turn heat to very low and simmer for 30 minutes. Add additional water as needed. Whisk in vinegar for last 10 minutes of cooking. Serve in bowls with hot rice. Garnish with minced raw onion.

Yield: 6 to 8 servings

Chapter Five

Plantains, Green Bananas and Other Caribbean Vegetables

Plantains, bananas, yautía, taro and all other sorts of vegetables grow freely in Puerto Rico. For those islanders who live in high-rises in San Juan, the grocery stores burst with a colorful selection of produce.

If you can't find plantains at a stateside grocery, give green bananas a try. I encourage all to experiment with at least a couple of the recipes in this chapter. Even though some of the vegetables seem odd or unpalatable, true Puerto Rican fare has not been experienced until you've had chayote, one of the root vegetables or plantain.

Plantain Stuffed with Garlic Shrimp
(Mofongo Rellenos con Camarones)

Puerto Ricans love their garlic and this recipe is no exception.

3 large plantains, peeled and
  soaked in salted water
1 large garlic clove, minced
1 tablespoon olive oil
1/4 pound pork crackling,
  chicharrón, well crumbled
1/3 cup chicken broth
vegetable oil or shortening for
  frying

Stuffing:
3 tablespoons olive oil
1/2 cup minced yellow onion
4 garlic cloves crushed
1/4 cup sofrito
3 tablespoons tomato paste
3 tablespoons dry sherry
2 pounds medium raw shrimp,
  deshelled, deveined and
  coarsely chopped

1. Slice plantains in diagonal 1-inch slices. Heat oil to 350°F.

2. In the meantime, sauté crushed garlic in olive oil, until soft, but not browned. Remove from heat.

3. Fry plantain slices a few at a time until golden, but still soft, not crunchy. Drain on white paper towels. Allow to cool slightly.

4. Run plantain slices through a food processor. Fold in garlic and pork crackling.

5. Form into small balls, about 1 1/2 inches in diameter. Set aside.

Stuffing:

1. Sauté the onion and garlic in the olive oil in a large skillet over moderate heat until soft, about 5 minutes. Do not brown.
2. Whisk in tomato paste, sofrito and sherry, simmering for 2 more minutes.
3. Drop in shrimp, and simmer, stirring constantly until shrimp turns pink. Remove from heat and allow to cool slightly.
4. Make a well in the center of each mofongo patty. Fill with shrimp, pinch mofongo shut over top. Serve warm with Mojito Sauce

Yield: about 10 balls

Traditional Shredded Green Plantain Fritters (Arañitas)

Serve with Mojito Sauce. If you don't have time to make it, serve with a mild or hot chili pepper sauce.

4 large green plantains, peeled, soaked and grated in shreds
1 teaspoon salt
1 teaspoon cracked black pepper

3 large garlic cloves, minced
vegetable oil or shortening for frying

Plantain

Plantains are related to bananas and native to Malaysia. Unlike bananas, plantains are eaten cooked, either from unripe or ripe fruit. Unripe fruit is green, ripe is yellow, turning to black.

Purchasing: Choose firm, unblemished skin. Black plantains do not always indicate spoilage, they are merely ripe.

Storing: Keep at room temperature. Refrigerate only if excessively ripe. Peel ripe plantains, wrap and freeze.

Serving: Unripe, cooked plantain is served as a starchy vegetable in soups and stews or as a side dish. Cooked ripe plantain tastes similar to sweet banana. Use as an accompaniment to fish, chicken or meat dishes.

Nutrition: Like its cousin, the banana, plantains are high in potassium. Also contains Vitamin C, Vitamin B-6, Vitamin A, folic acid and magnesium.

1. Preheat oil to 350°F.
2. Combine the shredded plantain with the salt, pepper and garlic, mixing well.
3. Scoop up a ping-pong sized ball of plantain and flatten between your palms.
4. Lower into hot oil and fry until golden. Do not overcrowd skillet as this will lower cooking temperature and cause fritters to soak up too much oil.
5. Remove with slotted spoon and drain on white paper towels.
6. Serve warm with Mojito Sauce.

Yield: about 12

Plantain and Meat Pie (Pastelón de Plátanos Maduros [Amarillos] con Carne)

Make two of these popular meat pies. They're sure to go fast.

1 1/2 cups Beef and Pork Filling
   for Piononos
6 large, partially ripe plantains,
   cut in half cross-wise
1 teaspoon salt

1 stick butter, chilled and
   chopped
3/4 cup flour
1/4 cup dry sherry

1. Preheat oven to 350°F. Generously grease a glass 9 or 10-inch pie dish with shortening. Set aside.
2. Bring 2 quarts water to boil along with the 1 teaspoon salt. Add unpeeled plantain halves and boil for 20 minutes. Remove, drain and cool. Run through food processor or mash by hand.
3. Cut butter into flour with a fork until crumbly resembling sand.
4. Fold into plantain mash, combining well.
5. Press half of plantain mixture into bottom of pie plate. Top with meat filling. Sprinkle sherry over meat.
6. Press remaining plantain mash over meat filling.
7. Bake for 30 minutes until lightlty browned.

Serves: 6

Spicy Sautéed Green Bananas

I'm not a huge fan of green bananas, but this recipe finally won me over. Nice and spicy.

10 medium size green bananas, boiled
4 tablespoons olive oil
1 medium yellow onion, thinly sliced
4 garlic cloves, minced
1 jalapeño or habañero pepper, seeded and minced (habañero, a.k.a. scotch bonnet is much hotter than the jalapeño)

4 tablespoons tomato paste
$^1/_4$ cup chicken broth
2 tablespoons vinegar
10 whole black peppercorns
10 pimento-stuffed olives, coarsely chopped
1 tablespoon capers
$^1/_4$ cup pimentos, chopped (canned is fine)
$^1/_3$ cup water

1. Sauté onion and garlic in the olive oil in a large skillet over moderate heat until soft, about 5 to 6 minutes.
2. Add hot peppers, tomato paste, chicken broth and vinegar. Simmer for 5 minutes.
3. Stir in peppercorns, olives, capers and pimentos, simmering for 10 minutes.
4. Add banana slices and simmer for additional 10 minutes.

Yield: 4 to 6 servings

Breadfruit Fritters
(Frituras de Panapén)

Be sure to serve this fritter at cocktail parties—it soaks up alcohol nicely.

2 cups warm, mashed breadfruit
1 tablespoon flour
3 tablespoons butter
1 garlic clove, crushed
2 large eggs, beaten

1 egg yolk, beaten
salt
pepper
vegetable oil or shortening for frying

1. Melt butter in small skillet over low heat. Sprinkle in flour and garlic. Cook for 3 minutes, stirring constantly to make a roux.
2. Fill a deep fryer or skillet with oil. Heat to 350°F.

3. Fold roux into mashed breadfruit. Stir in eggs, combining well.

4. Drop by spoonfuls into hot oil. Be careful not too overcrowd pan.

5. Remove with slotted spoon. Drain on white paper towels. Serve as appetizer or side dish. Season to taste with salt and pepper.

Yield: about 12 fritters

Garlic Pepper Cassava Fries
(Yuca con Mojo de Ajo)

These fries were habit forming. I made Anna take them all home with her.

3 pounds cassava (yucca), peeled and cut in $3^{1}/_{2}$-inch by $^{3}/_{8}$-inch strips (fries)
1 teaspoon salt
5 large garlic cloves, minced

1 tablespoon cracked black pepper
2 tablespoons olive oil
vegetable oil for frying
salt

1. Fill a deep kettle with cold water and the 1 teaspoon salt. Bring to boil over medium-high heat.

2. Boil cassava strips for 20 minutes. Do not overcook as "fries" need to be firm.

3. Heat olive oil in a small frying pan. Sauté garlic and black pepper for 5 minutes. Remove from heat and set aside.

4. Fill a deep skillet or fryer with vegetable oil. Heat to 350°F. Fry cassava strips, one layer at a time, taking care not to overload or crowd skillet. Remove when golden and drain on white paper towels.

5. Drizzle garlic/pepper oil over "fries." Season to taste with salt and pepper.

Yield: 6 servings

Gingered Sweet Potatoes
(Batatas en Almíbar)

This is one of my favorite dishes to serve with roast turkey at holiday time.

3 pounds sweet potatoes,
  scrubbed and rinsed
1 tablespoon freshly grated
  ginger root

1/2 cup sugar
1/2 cup brown sugar
1/4 cup butter, melted
1/4 teaspoon ground nutmeg

1. Fill a large saucepan with water and bring to boiling point over high heat. Add sweet potatoes, reduce heat to moderate, cover and boil for 30 minutes. Remove and drain. Preheat oven to 350°F. Lightly oil a glass or ceramic baking dish.
2. Arrange a layer of sweet potato across bottom of dish. Spread grated ginger evenly over sweet potato. Sprinkle sugars over top. Drizzle melted butter over sugar.
3. Bake for 30 minutes.

Yield: 6 servings

Puerto Rican Pumpkin Pudding
(Budín de Calabaza)

I serve pumpkin pudding as a side dish to roast turkey, beef or pork, along with a green vegetable, rice and salad.

1 1/2 pounds West Indian
  pumpkin, or any other dry
  pumpkin or orange squash
  (butternut)
1 tablespoon salt

6 eggs, separated
1/2 teaspoon ground ginger
1/4 teaspoon nutmeg
1/4 cup brown sugar
4 tablespoons butter

1. Fill a deep kettle with cold water and 1 tablespoon salt. Bring to boil over medium-high heat.
2. Peel, seed and coarsely chop pumpkin. Boil pumpkin, uncovered, for 25 minutes until just tender. Remove from heat, drain and allow to cool somewhat.
3. Mash pumpkin or run through food processor. You will want a smooth, lump-free puree.

4. Preheat oven to 375°F. Butter a 2-quart glass or ceramic baking dish. Set aside.

5. Fold in beaten egg yolks, ginger, nutmeg, brown sugar and butter.

6. Beat egg whites until stiff peaks form.

7. Carefully fold into pumpkin mixture until barely blended.

8. Scoop into baking dish and bake for 30 minutes until golden.

Yield: 8 servings

Garlic Cheese Stuffed Chayotes
(Chayotes Rellenos con Queso y Ajo)

Chayotes is a light green, avocado-size and shaped vegetables that tastes a lot like zucchini, which you may substitute for the chayote. Serve with crusty bread and a crisp, green salad.

3 large chayotes, cut in half, lengthwise

2 teaspoons salt

1 tablespoon olive oil

4 garlic cloves, minced

2 tablespoons minced onion

1 1/4 cups shredded sharp cheese, such as Cheddar or Gouda

1/2 cup unseasoned bread crumbs

2 tablespoons melted butter

La Mina Falls in El Yunque, Caribbean National Forest

1. Fill a medium saucepan with water and salt. Bring to a boil and add chayotes. Reduce heat and boil for 20 to 30 minutes, until soft.
2. Remove from heat and allow to cool slightly. Remove pulp, discarding cores and stringy part. Reserve unbroken shells.
3. Mash chayote and set aside.
4. Preheat oven to 350°F.
5. Sauté garlic and minced onion in the olive oil in a small frying pan over moderate heat, until soft. Do not brown. Remove from heat.
6. Place cheese in a medium bowl and fold in garlic mixture, stirring well. Cut in shredded cheese, until combined. Fold in mashed chayote.
7. Stuff shells with garlic/cheese/chayote filling.
8. Using the same frying pan for the garlic, add breadcrumbs and melted butter. Stir over low heat for 1 minute. Remove from heat.
9. Top stuffed shells with breadcrumb mixture. Place in oven and bake for 30 minutes.

Yield: 6 servings

Flamboyant tree

Chapter Six

Seafood

Seafood is available in abundance in Puerto Rico with the Atlantic Ocean on one side and the Caribbean on the other. Many of the typical seafood dishes show the Spanish heritage of the island, many using sofrito as their base.

West coast beach

Fried Fish with Mojito Sauce
(Pescado Frito Con Mojito Isleño)

This delicious, traditional dish originated from the island's coastal towns, but has gained popularity inland. Mojito Isleño comes from Salinas.

3¹/₂ pounds firm white fish fillets (cod, snapper, flounder, turbo, etc.) ³/₄ inch thick

2 teaspoons salt

Mojito:

¹/₄ cup, plus 1 tablespoon olive oil

2 large yellow onions, thinly sliced

1 can (8 ounce) tomato sauce

4 tablespoons tomato paste

3 tablespoons cider vinegar

1¹/₄ cups water

¹/₃ cup alcaparrado

1 large bay leaf

2 teaspoons freshly cracked black pepper

1¹/₂ teaspoons salt

2 roasted red peppers or pimentos, sliced in strips

vegetable oil for frying

2 cloves garlic, peeled and chopped coarsely

1. Rinse fish fillets under cold running water. Pat dry, season with salt. Set aside.

2. Heat olive oil in a large saucepan over medium heat. Sauté onion slices for 7 minutes. Do not brown. Remove from heat.

3. Stir together tomato sauce, tomato paste, vinegar and water in a medium bowl until well combined. Pour into sauce pan and stir.

4. Fold in alcaparrado, bay leaf, black pepper, salt and black pepper, roasted pepper or pimento strips. Return to low to medium heat, cover and simmer for 20 minutes. Uncover and simmer for additional 20 minutes. Remove from heat, cover and keep in a warm place.

5. Heat ¹/₂ inch of vegetable oil in a large skillet. Stir in garlic. Carefully lower fish fillets into hot oil. Do not overcrowd skillet. Fry over medium heat, 3¹/₂ minutes on each side. Fish should be cooked through in center, flaking easily with a fork.

6. Transfer to a serving platter, drizzling mojito sauce over top. Serve with plantains, okra and a green salad.

Yield: 4 to 6 servings

Tip – Fish

* To remove the stubborn odor of fish from the air and a pan, combine equal parts of vinegar and water and boil for 10 minutes.

* To thaw frozen fish quickly, place in a zippered plastic bag and place in a sink full of cold water.

* To loosen fish stuck to a pan, drizzle a small amount of oil into the pan, swirl and gently loosen.

Stewed Shrimp (Camarones Guisados)

Puerto Ricans love their garlic, and this recipe is no exception. Serve with crisp green salad and ice-cold beer.

5 whole black peppercorns
4 large garlic cloves, peeled and coarsely chopped
1 teaspoon salt
2 fresh culantro leaves or 2 tablespoons minced cilantro
2 tablespoons olive oil
1 medium yellow onion, minced
2 green frying peppers, seeded and minced
1 16-ounce can plum tomatoes, liquid and all
1 tablespoon tomato paste

3 tablespoons sherry
1 tablespoon apple cider vinegar
1 bay leaf
$1/4$ teaspoon dried thyme
1 teaspoon salt
$1/4$ cup alcaparrado
2 pounds raw shrimp, shelled and deveined

1. Grind together black peppercorns, garlic and salt in a mortar and pestle. For best results, use an up and down motion. Add cilantro, mashing well. Set aside.

2. Heat olive oil in a large skillet. Sauté onions and peppers for 2 minutes over moderate heat.

3. Stir in plum tomatoes, tomato paste, sherry, vinegar and bay leaf. Simmer for 5 minutes. Stir in thyme and salt. Fold in alcaparrado.

4. Add shrimp and cook, uncovered, until pink. Serve over rice.

Yield: 6 servings

Spicy Shrimp and Chorizo in Beer
(Camarones en Cerveza)

I don't think I've ever come across a cuisine or cookbook that didn't have sort sort of recipe for shrimp and beer. The chorizo gives it a Latin twist.

1 1/2 cups beer
1/2 cup sofrito
1 6-inch chorizo, crumbled
2 pounds fresh or frozen
   shrimp, shelled, but tails on

2 tablespoons butter
2 tablespoons flour

1. Blend beer and sofrito in a large bowl. Stir in shrimp and chorizo. Marinate overnight.

2. Melt butter over low heat in a small saucepan. Sprinkle in flour, stirring constantly until lightly browned. Remove roux from heat and set aside.

3. Pour into large kettle and bring beer and shrimp to a boil. Whisk in roux, reduce heat, cook and uncovered for 10 minutes until sauce has thickened.

4. Serve over hot rice, with okra and plantains.

Yield: 6 servings

Crab Stewed in Marsala and Plum Tomatoes (Jueyes Criolla)

If you don't have access to fresh crabmeat, canned will do in a pinch. Be sure to pick out any stones or cartilage.

5 black pepper corns
3 garlic cloves, peeled and
   coarsely chopped
1 teaspoon salt
1/2 teaspoon oregano
1/4 teaspoon cumin
1/4 teaspoon nutmeg
2 tablespoons olive oil
1 teaspoon annatto oil

1/2 cup minced yellow onion
1 small green frying pepper,
   seeded and minced
1/2 cup Marasala wine
1 16-ounce can plum tomatoes,
   1/2 cup liquid reserved
1 tablespoon tomato paste
1 1/2 cups boiled crab meat

1. Grind the peppercorns, garlic, salt, oregano, cumin and nutmeg in a mortar and pestle until smooth. Set aside.

2. Heat olive and annatto oil in a deep kettle or large saucepan over medium heat. Sauté onion and pepper for 5 minutes until soft, but not brown.

3. Whisk in wine. Chop plum tomatoes coarsely and add to saucepan along with half a cup of liquid from can. Stir in tomato paste and simmer for 5 minutes.

4. Add flaked crab meat, stir, reduce heat, cover and cook for 12 minutes.

Yield: 4 servings

Lighthouse in Fajardo

Chapter Seven

Chicken and Turkey

Did you know that more chickens than people exist in the world? Chicken is the world's largest source of animal protein, with the United States alone producing over 5 billion chickens are year. Probably a good thing when you consider how much of our natural resources are utilized to turn out a pound of beef.

At one time, most island homes had a chicken coop located near the house. This furnished the family with eggs and meat and a feathered 'watch-dog'. The sound of someone walking would rouse the entire chicken coop and alert the household.

Today, chicken coops have diminished in number. Coamo is home to the majority of the island's poultry-raising farms. However, chicken is still a staple of the Puerto Rican diet. The most well-known dish being Arroz Con Pollo.

Friendly local iguana

Chicken and Rice (Arroz con Pollo)

Enjoy this traditional island recipe with fried plantain and sliced tomatoes drizzled with olive oil and vinegar.

1 3-lb chicken, cut into serving pieces
2 tablespoons adobo
4 tablespoons olive oil, divided
2 tablespoons annatto oil
1/2 cup recaíto
1/3 cup sofrito
2 ounces cured ham, diced
12 pimento-stuffed olives
1 tablespoon, plus 1 teaspoon capers

1 tablespoon tomato paste
1 tablespoon wine vinegar
1 tablespoon dry sherry
2 cups hot chicken broth
1 1/2 cups hot water
3 cups long-grain rice
1 10-ounce can pigeon peas or green peas
1/2 cup roasted pimentos, canned or bottled fine

1. Rinse and pat dry chicken pieces. Rub with adobo seasoning.
2. Heat 2 tablespoons of the olive oil in a large skillet. Brown chicken on all sides. Remove from heat, drain and set aside.
3. Heat annatto and olive oil in a large saucepan or deep skillet over moderate heat. Sauté recaíto for 5 minutes, stirring occasionally.
4. Fold in sofrito, ham, olives, capers, tomato paste, vinegar and sherry, cooking for another 2 minutes.
5. Pour in chicken broth and water to recaíto mixture. Stir in rice, then peas, then chicken pieces.
6. Turn heat up to medium and cook, uncovered, until liquid reaches top of rice.
7. Fork over rice from top to bottom. Reduce heat, cover and simmer for 30 minutes.
8. Fork over rice again, cover and cook for 5 more minutes. Remove from heat. Garnish with pimento strips, cover and allow to sit for 5 minutes.

Yield: 8 to 10 servings

Palmas del Mar

Roast Turkey with Criolla Stuffing
(Pavo Relleno a la Criolla)

Serve this highly-seasoned island bird with rice and pigeon peas, Puerto Rican style. Note: before you place turkey on a rack, cover the rack with heavily greased foil to keep the skin from tearing when you turn the bird.

1 eight to nine pound turkey
8 cloves garlic, peeled
2 teaspoons cracked black pepper
1 tablespoon dried oregano
1 tablespoon salt
1/4 cup olive oil
2 tablespoons paprika
2 tablespoons fresh chopped thyme, or 1 tablespoon dried
3 tablespoons cider or wine vinegar

4 tablespoons olive oil
1 1/2 pounds lean ground beef
1 cup minced onion
1/2 cup sofrito
1/4 cup chopped alcaparrado
1/2 cup seedless raisins
1 cup applesauce
3 hard-boiled eggs, chopped
2 bottles of beer

1. Rinse and wash turkey, inside and out. Pat dry. Rinse and chop liver—this will be added to stuffing later.

2. Pound garlic, pepper, oregano and salt in a mortar until smooth. Mix in olive oil, paprika, thyme and vinegar. Rub garlic mixture inside and out of turkey. Cover turkey and refrigerate overnight.

3. Heat 3 tablespoons of the olive oil in a large skillet over medium heat. Brown meat lightly. Drain and set aside in a heat-proof dish.

4. Heat remaining tablespoon of olive oil over moderate heat. Sauté onions for 5 minutes until soft, but not browned. Stir in sofrito, alcaparrado and raisins, cooking for 5 minutes.

5. Return meat to pan and simmer for 5 minutes. Remove from heat. Fold in applesauce and eggs. Allow to cool.

6. Preheat oven to 325°F. Remove turkey from refrigerator and stuff three-quarters full. Truss turkey.

7. Place turkey, breast down, on roasting rack, covered with heavily greased foil. Poke a couple of holes in the foil to allow the fat and juices to drain to the bottom of the pan.

8. Pour beer into bottom of pan. Roast turkey for 2 to 2 1/2 hours. See note above for cooking times. Baste turkey every 20 minutes with beer and drippings. Turn breast up after one hour. If you've chosen a bird heavier than 12 pounds, turn breast up after 1 1/2 hours.

9. Turkey is down when the drumstick and thigh move easily. Or when the temperature of the breast meat (use a meat thermometer) reads 170°F and the thigh is at 180°F. Place turkey on large platter and cover loosely with foil. Allow to sit 15 minutes before carving.

Yield: 8 to 9 servings (figure one pound of bird per serving)

Tip – Cooking Times for Turkey

Cook 15 minutes per pound if bird weighs less than 16 pounds. Twelve minutes per pound if heavier.

Vieques

Taste of Puerto Rico

Chapter Eight

Beef and Pork

Pre-Colombian Puerto Rico did not have any livestock, except a few iguanas and small dogs. The Spaniards changed that when they brought over sheep, cattle, pigs, rabbits and fowl.

Beef and pork have been part of the Puerto Rican menu for centuries. Roast suckling pig is a national holiday tradition. Steak smothered in onions is an everyday delight. Stuffed pot roast is another favorite.

Serve these meat dishes alongside plantain and green banana recipes, rice, beans and other Caribbean vegetables.

Secluded beach on north east coast of Puerto Rico

Puerto Rican Steak and Onions
(Biftec Encebollado)

*This is the traditional steak and onions dish Puerto Rico is famous for.
Note: season the meat and marinate in the refrigerator for a couple days.*

2 pounds boneless sirloin or
   beef round, thinly sliced
1 1/2 teaspoons salt
1 teaspoon freshly cracked
   black pepper
4 garlic cloves, peeled and
   crushed

3 tablespoons olive oil
2 medium yellow onions, thinly
   sliced
extra olive oil for sautéing
2 tablespoons dry sherry

1. Trim any fat or gristle from meat. Pound lightly with a wooden mallet to thin. Rub with salt.

2. Combine pepper and garlic. Rub into meat. Arrange onion slices over top and drizzle with olive oil.

3. Cover and refrigerate for several hours, overnight if possible.

4. Heat about 1/4-inch of the extra olive oil in a large, heavy-bottomed skillet over medium heat. Sauté meat slices one minute on each side. Set meat aside.

5. Drain nearly all the olive oil from pan. Sauté the onion slices until soft, about 5 minutes. Remove from pan and arrange on top of meat.

6. Deglaze pan by adding sherry, stirring up bits of brown. Simmer for 2 to 3 minutes.

7. Pour over meat and onions. Serve with hot white rice, plantains and okra.

Yield: 6 servings

Shredded Beef Stew (Ropa Vieja)

Ropa Vieja has echoes of the Spanish past. Despite the title, translating literally to 'old rags', this recipe yields a tender and flavorful beef stew. Note: Buy a steak or roast from the chuck and cube it yourself. Those prepackaged cuts of stew beef are made up of odds and ends of different muscle sections that couldn't be sold otherwise. Because of the inconsistencies, the meat will cook at different times. Cut all your own meat from the same cut to ensure even flavor and cooking times.

2 pounds beef chuck, trimmed and cut in 1 1/2 inch cubes
1 carrot
1 large onion, halved
1/2 cup red wine
1/2 teaspoon salt
3 tablespoons olive oil
2 yellow onions, thinly sliced
2 cloves garlic, peeled and minced

1 large green frying pepper, seeded and minced
2 large tomatoes, peeled and chopped, about 2 cups
2 tablespoons tomato paste
1 bay leaf
1/4 teaspoon ground allspice
1/4 teaspoon ground oregano
salt and freshly cracked black pepper to taste

1. Place the beef, along with the carrot, onion halves, red wine and salt in a large saucepan with sufficient water to cover. Simmer over low heat, covered, for 1 1/2 hours. Remove from heat and allow to cool.
2. Shred meat, reserving stock. Set aside.
3. Heat olive oil in a large, heavy frying pan. Sauté onion, garlic and frying pepper until soft, but not brown.
4. Stir in tomatoes, tomato paste, bay leaf, allspice and oregano. Simmer until thickened, about 30 minutes.
5. Add 2 cups of reserved stock and shredded meat. Simmer for 15 minutes. Serve with rice and beans or mashed breadfruit.

Yield: 6 servings

Churrasco with Chimichurri Sauce

Churrasco is a Spanish term referring to grilled meat, differing in preparation style across Latin America and Europe. In Puerto Rico, churrasco is a skirt or flank steak, in Nicaragua it is a tenderloin, and in Chile, churrasco is a thin cut of steak served on a toasted bun. What really makes the churrasco is the wonderful chimichurri sauce made from olive oil, parsley, spices and copious amounts of garlic. Make the sauce the night before and marinate the meat to meld the flavors.

8 large garlic cloves, crushed
1 1/2 cups fresh parsley, coarsely chopped
1/2 cup fresh cilantro, coarsely chopped

1/4 cup fresh oregano, stripped, coarsely chopped
2–3 jalapeño peppers, seeded and chopped (more or less to taste)

1 cup extra-virgin olive oil
1/3 cup white vinegar
1/4 cup water (use more or less
   to adjust thickness of sauce)
1 1/2 teaspoons salt

1 teaspoon fresh cracked black
   pepper
4 (6 to 8-ounce) pieces of flank
   or skirt steak

1. Combine all ingredients for chimichurri sauce, except the vinegar,
   and puree in a food processor until smooth. Stir in vinegar. Baste
   the meat with the sauce, reserving half for later dipping.
   Refrigerate meat and extra sauce for at least four hours.

2. Set up the grill and preheat to high. Grill steaks until desired
   doneness and allow meat to rest for five minutes before serving.
   Serve with remaining chimichurri sauce on the side.

Yield: 4 servings

Tip–Pot Roast

When I experimented with the pot roasts, I wanted something that would
not be tough and dry on the outside and rare inside. Roasting at 250° for
the first hour cooked the meat on the inside. Turning up to 500° for
15 minutes, browned the outside nicely.

Roast Pork Leg with Sherry Gravy
(Pernil Al Horno)

*Instead of the traditional turkey that is served at Christmas or
Thanksgiving on the mainland, Puerto Ricans prepare roast pork. Serve
with rice and pigeon peas.*

1 4 to 6 pound pork leg
juice of one lemon
8 large garlic cloves, sliced
8 peppercorns
2 teaspoons dried whole
   oregano
2 tablespoons olive oil

2 tablespoons cider or malt
   vinegar
1 teaspoon salt for each pound
   of pork
1/2 cup dry sherry
1/4 cup flour

1. Rinse pork under cold running water. Pat dry with paper towels.
   Squeeze lemon juice over entire leg. This will do much to alleviate
   the 'porkish' odor.

2. Cut slits in the skin and fat using the tip of a sharp knife. Insert garlic slices into skin.

3. Crush peppercorns in a mortar. Mash in salt, vinegar and olive oil. Rub this into meat.

4. Refrigerate overnight. Remove from refrigerator $1/2$ hour before cooking time. Preheat oven to 300°.

5. Transfer meat to a roasting pan. Insert a meat thermometer into center of meat. Bake for 2 hours. Meat should be golden.

6. Turn oven up to 350°. Bake for another 45 minutes. Thermometer should read 185°F. Remove from oven and place on large cutting board.

7. Meanwhile, to make gravy, drain liquid from roasting pan into a glass measuring cup. Skim off fat, measure off $1/4$ cup and reserve. You should have $2^{1/2}$ cups of juices left over. If you don't have enough liquid, add water. If not enough fat, add butter to make up the $1/4$ cup.

8. Pour liquid into a medium saucepan, stirring in sherry over medium-high heat. Bring to a boil.

9. Heat fat in a small skillet and whisk in flour over medium-high heat to make a roux. Stir fat into hot liquid, smoothing out any lumps. Reduce heat and cook until gravy has thickened. Remove from heat. Pour over sliced pork roast.

Yield: 6 to 8 servings

Sugarcane and Ginger Pork Chops
(Chuletas de Cerdo Rebozadas con Jengibre)

Columbus brought sugar cane from the Canary Islands on his second voyage to the New World in 1493. Subsequently, slaves were brought over to work the sugar cane fields in the early 16th century. The rum industry was born on Puerto Rico.

6 pork chops, cut $1/2$-inch thick, trimmed
4 garlic cloves, peeled and crushed
$1^{1/2}$ teaspoons cracked black peppercorns
$1^{1/2}$ teaspoons salt
$1/4$ teaspoon ground cinnamon

$1/4$ teaspoon ground cardamom
1 tablespoon butter
1 tablespoon olive oil
$1/4$ cup minced yellow onion
$1/2$ cup packed light brown sugar
$3/4$ cup chicken broth
$1/4$ cup dark rum

¹/₄ cup sweet white wine

2 tablespoons butter

1 tablespoon grated fresh
   ginger

1 teaspoon lemon juice

1. Rinse the chops under cold running water. Pat dry.

2. Combine the black pepper corns, garlic, salt, cinnamon and cardamom in a small bowl. Rub the meat with this. Allow to marinate 1 hour in the refrigerator.

3. Melt butter in a 10- to 12-inch skillet over medium-high heat. Add oil and swirl until fat browns slightly and begins to smoke.

4. Place chops in skillet and brown, about 1 minute. Turn and brown on other side for 1 minute.

5. Reduce heat to moderate, cover and cook for 4 minutes. Flip chops over and cook for 4¹/₂ additional minutes. Chops should be firm, but not hard. Transfer chops to serving dish and keep in a warm place.

6. Drain all but 2 tablespoons of the fat from the skillet. Sauté onion until soft, about 1 minute. Add sugar, stirring rapidly for 1 minute. Stir in broth, rum and wine. Boil until reduced by half, about 1¹/₂ minutes. Stir in ginger and cook for 3 minutes. You should have a syrup by now.

7. Remove from heat, swirl in 1 tablespoon butter. Drizzle in lemon juice, swirling again.

8. Spoon over pork chops.

Yield: 6 servings

Parque de Bombas, Ponce

Taste of Puerto Rico

Chapter Nine

Flans, Custards and Puddings

Puerto Rico has an incredibly varied selection of decadently rich flans and custards. It's no surprise as each wave of immigrants, Spanish, Danish, French and English, contributed recipes from their home country. Luscious tropical fruits, eggs from free-range hens, locally grown sugar cane and aromatic spices, inspired many new variations on old favorites.

This chapter contains a range of velvety desserts meant to be eaten with a spoon—everything from the island's most popular dessert, flan, to tembleque, a coconut custard to isles flotante (floating islands), a meringue garnished dessert.

Traditional Flan

Technically speaking, a flan is an open tart with a sweet or tangy filling. But, in Puerto Rico, and in other Latin countries, flan is a baked custard. Often cooked in a *baine-marie*, the custard is poured into a mold, then placed and cooked in a pan of hot water reaching halfway up the sides of the mold.

Glazing caramel:

1 cup white granulated sugar

Flan:

1 cup whole milk
1 cup evaporated milk
1 cup sweetened condensed milk

3/4 cup white granulated sugar
1/2 teaspoon salt
7 whole large eggs at room temperature, plus 1 additional yolk,
2 teaspoons vanilla extract
1/4 teaspoon ground cinnamon
1/4 teaspoon ground nutmeg

1. Glazing caramel: place the 1 cup sugar in a heavy skillet over low heat. Stir continuously with a wooden spoon until sugar melts. Continue to stir and cook until sugar darkens. Do not make too dark as this impart a bitter taste.

2. Pour caramel into 8 to 10 heat-resistant custard molds or ramekins. Tip the sides if desired, ensuring that caramel coats evenly. Set aside to cool.

3. Preheat oven to 350°F. Add water to baine-marie mold or a large glass baking dish so that water reaches 2/3 up the sides of flan molds. Place in oven to begin heating water.

4. Whisk together milks, sugar and salt in a saucepan. Do not allow to foam. Scald over medium high heat. Do not boil. Remove from heat and set aside. Allow to cool to nearly room temperature.

5. Beat eggs and yolks lightly in a medium bowl. Do not allow to foam as this will result in a sandy-textured flan. Add scalded milk and strain for lumps.

6. Fold in vanilla, cinnamon and nutmeg. Pour into caramelized mold and set in the pan of hot water in oven.

7. Bake for 45 minutes until done. Flan that is done will jiggle like Jello® when done.

8. Remove from oven and pan of water. Cool for 2 hours before serving. Refrigerate covered.

9. To serve, invert onto a serving dish.

Yield: 8 to 10 servings

Cheese Flan (Flan de Queso)

Cheese Flan is my favorite. I like to serve this with fresh raspberries.

$3/4$ cup sugar to caramelize a mold

4 ounces softened cream cheese (room temperature)

1/2 cup granulated sugar

$1/4$ teaspoon salt

6 ounces evaporated milk

6 ounces sweetened condensed milk

$1/2$ cup water

6 large eggs, room temperature

2 teaspoons vanilla extract

$1/2$ teaspoon ground ginger

1. Caramelize flan mold as instructed in Basic Vanilla Flan recipe. Set aside.

2. Preheat oven to 350°F. Fill a large glass baking dish with water to come up 2/3 height of the flan mold. Set in oven to heat water.

3. Beat cream cheese and sugar by hand or with an electric mixer set on low until smooth.

4. Combine salt, milks, water, eggs and vanilla in a separate small bowl. Stir in ginger.

5. Beat milk mixture into cheese mixture. Blend well. Spoon into mold.

6. Place into water bath and bake for 45 minutes. Cover with aluminum foil to prevent excessive browning of top and bake additional 45 minutes. A toothpick inserted in center should come out clean.

7. Cool for 2 hours and then refrigerate.

8. Run a wet knife around rim and invert onto a serving platter. Slice into wedges.

Yield: 8 to 10 servings

Coconut Flan with Mango Sauce
(Flan de Coco con Salsa de Mango)

While on a photo shoot with my husband (now ex) and photographer Buddy Moffet, we stayed at the El Convento Hotel in Old San Juan. This was before the hotel was remodeled. Buddy and Richard decided to hit the casinos in Isla Verde and I ordered room service. I ordered flan for the first time. The mango sauce served alongside began my love affair with flan.

Caramel

Sugar, heated, will turn to caramel, first a light golden color, then brown, then black (overdone). The darker the caramel, the more intense the flavor.

Correct temperature: For best results, use a candy thermometer between 320°F for a light flavor, 350°F for a deeper, more intense flavor.

Even cooking: Begin with low heat, and no stirring, until sugar has completely melted. Bring to a boil only after the sugar has melted. Do not stir once boiling has commenced. Shake pan back and forth while cooking. Once cooked, remove from heat and transfer to a clean, heat proof container. Place over a simmer pot of hot water to keep warm.

Caramelizing molds: When glazing custard ramekins or molds, have a bowl of ice water on hand in case any of the melted sugar should spill on your hand. Anna and I discovered it's not necessary to tip and coat the sides of the molds. Dangerous at best. Once I ended up with a scorch mark on my stomach. Just pour a little extra caramel into the bottom of the ramekin. When the flan is inverted, it will run down the sides anyway.

Clean up: Always the fun part. Do not let caramel cool and harden in pan. If it does, add water to pan and simmer over low heat.

1 cup granulated sugar to caramelize a mold
1¾ cups sugar
1 cup, plus 2 tablespoons water
2¼ cups freshly grated coconut
1 teaspoon freshly grated lime zest
9 eggs, room temperature and lightly beaten
2 medium mangoes, peeled, seeded, puréed, and pressed through a sieve to remove strings and fibers
1 tablespoon fresh lime juice
2 tablespoons dark or gold rum

1. Caramelize a 7- to 9-inch flan mold as per Basic Vanilla Flan recipe. Set aside.

2. Place water and sugar in a medium saucepan over high heat and bring to boil for 30 minutes. Mixture should be brought to a thread-stage syrup, about 230°F on a candy thermometer. Remove from heat.

3. Preheat oven to 325°F and fill a glass baking dish with water to come up ²/₃ the height of the flan mold. Place inside oven to heat water.

4. Stir in coconut and lime zest to sugar mixture. Reduce heat enough so that eggs will not curdle when added. Add eggs, combine well, and strain into flan mold.

5. Set in hot water bath in oven and bake for 1 to 1½ hours until firm. A toothpick inserted in center will come out clean.

El Convento, Old San Juan

6. Allow to cool for 2 hours. Run a wet knife around rim, then invert on a serving platter.
7. Combine puréed mango, lime juice and rum. Pour over top of flan. Serve at once.

Yield: 8 to 10 servings

Coconut Custard (Tembleque)

The word tembleque translates to "shaky". I've had this desert in an Ocean Park (near Isla Verde and Condado in San Juan) restaurant served in a small plastic flower pot with a silk flower inserted in the center. The "soil" on top was made from crushed oreo cookies. This dessert is often served at Christmas.

4 cups fresh coconut milk or
　unsweetened canned coconut
　milk
1 teaspoon vanilla extract

²/₃ cup sugar
³/₄ teaspoon salt
6 tablespoons cornstarch
ground nutmeg

Taste of Puerto Rico

1. Whirl all ingredients in a blender until smooth and free of lumps. Allow foam to subside and scoop off excess.
2. Pour into a medium saucepan and bring to a boil over medium heat.
3. Reduce heat and simmer until thickened, about 3 to 4 minutes. The custard should coat the back of a spoon when ready.
4. Pour into individual custard molds. Sprinkle lightly with nutmeg. Cover snugly with plastic wrap else a skin will form. Refrigerate over night.

Yield: 6 servings

Spiced Pumpkin and Coconut Pudding (Cazuela)

This was a very interesting and delicious dessert to make. It contains pumpkin, sweet potatoes, ginger, cinnamon and anise combined with fresh coconut milk—a heady combination.

My Puerto Rican friend Anna explained to me that a cazuela is an earthenware pot or casserole used to cook food. The clay actually imparts an earthenware taste to food. I know that certain health food aficionados advocate eating clay for its vital minerals and health benefits. Perhaps cooking in a clay pot does the same. Let's hope.

2 pounds pumpkin or butternut squash, peeled, seeded and cut into 2-inch cubes
2 pounds sweet potatoes, peeled, seeded and cut into 2-inch cubes
1 tablespoon salt
$1/2$ cup water
1 tablespoon freshly grated ginger
1 teaspoon freshly grated lime zest
1 teaspoon star anise or $1/2$ teaspoon ground anise
1 cinnamon stick

4 whole cloves
$1/4$ teaspoon ground nutmeg
6 tablespoon butter, softened
4 large eggs, beaten
$1 1/2$ cups, plus 1 tablespoon sugar
5 tablespoons all-purpose flour
1 cup fresh coconut milk
1 teaspoon vanilla extract
1 teaspoon sea salt
$1/4$ teaspoon black pepper
2 tablespoons butter
plantain leaves (substitute parchment if not available), washed and patted dry.

1. Fill a large pot with pumpkin and sweet potato. Fill and cover with water and the 1 tablespoon salt. Cover and bring to a boil over medium heat for 35 minutes or until vegetables are soft. Drain water.

2. Stir together the $^1/_2$ cup water, ginger, lime zest, anise, cinnamon, cloves, and ground nutmeg in a small saucepot. Cover, bring to boil, reduce heat and simmer for 5 minutes. Strain through a mesh sieve. Reserve liquid and discard spices.

3. Mash slightly cooled pumpkin and sweet potato by hand. Stir in reserved spice liquid.

4. Fold in butter, eggs, and sugar. Whisk in flour, coconut milk, vanilla, salt and black pepper.

5. Preheat oven to 350°F.

6. Butter an 8- to 10-inch earthenware casserole dish with 1 tablespoon of the butter. Line the dish with the plantain leaves, buttering these as well.

7. Scoop pumpkin mixture onto leaves, cover loosely with foil and bake for $1^1/_2$ hours.

8. Cool on wire rack for 2 hours. Invert on serving dish, removing plantain leaves.

Yield: 12 servings

Tip – Cornstarch in Custards

* Custards made with cornstarch can be heated above 180° without curdling. Starch molecules keep egg protein molecules from clumping together.

* Use cornstarch with chocolate or other heavily flavored puddings only. The flavorings mask the cornstarch texture which can become somewhat grainy.

* Cornstarch sets custards quite firmly, so is not suitable for flan, which needs to be jiggly.

Guava Bread Pudding
(Budín de Pan y Guayaba)

The fruit of the guava tree, native to tropical America, is part of the myrtle family, along with cinnamon, nutmeg and eucalyptus. It has a perfumey fragrance and a slight acid taste, making it a light and refreshing fruit. Guava is popular in many desserts in Puerto Rico.

3 cups whole milk
1 cups heavy cream
4 tablespoons butter
2 cups sugar
6 egg yolks, reserving whites
    for meringue
6 whole eggs
1 tablespoon dark rum
$1/2$ teaspoon salt

1 pound good quality white
    American loaf bread, crust
    trimmed and cut in 1-inch
    cubes
1 pound canned or jarred
    guava paste
6 egg whites
$1/2$ cup sugar

1. Preheat oven to 275°. Grease a 13- by 9-inch glass baking dish generously with butter.

2. Bring milk and heavy cream to a boil in medium saucepan. Remove from heat at once and stir in butter and sugar.

3. Beat the 6 eggs yolks along with the 6 whole eggs slightly. Add rum and salt. Gradually pour into milk mixture.

4. Line glass baking dish with bread cubes and pour milk/egg mixture over top. Bake $1^1/2$ hours. Remove from oven, but leave oven on.

5. Slice guava paste into thin slices and arrange over top of pudding.

6. Beat egg white until stiff, slowly whisking in the $1/2$ cup sugar. Spoon over guava slice and return to oven. Bake for additional 30 minutes.

7. Cool on wire rack. May be served with scoop of vanilla ice cream on side.

Yield: 8 servings

Chapter Ten

Sweet Treats: Cakes, Pies, Cookies, Candy and Ice Cream

The sweet tooth of Puerto Ricans has been influenced by various immigrants over the centuries: the Spanish, French, Danish, even the British. European heritage can be seen in the custards, puddings and flans, cheese-based desserts and pastries.

Tropical fruits, always in abundance on the island, made its way into many of the recipes, adding a refreshing touch. The recipes here are easy to duplicate, many of the tropical fruits readily found in mainland grocery stores.

East coast beach

Tres Leches Cake (Three Milk Cake)

Soaked in three different types of milk, this intensely flavored vanilla cake has suddenly taken the U.S. mainland, particularly Texas, by storm. The whipped cream topping, instead of a sugary frosting is divine.

Note: you'll need three medium-size mixing bowls and one large one. Rinse a medium bowl while the cake is baking for the whipped cream and chill it.

Cake:

8 large eggs, room temperature
1 1/2 cups, plus 1 tablespoon sugar
12 tablespoons butter, softened
1 3/4 cups, plus 3 tablespoons all-purpose flour
2 teaspoons baking powder
1 cup whole milk
2 teaspoons vanilla extract
1 teaspoon cream of tartar

Three milks:

8 ounces light cream
1 5-ounce can evaporated milk, room temperature
1 14-ounce can sweetened condensed milk, room temperature

Topping:

2 cups heavy cream
1/4 cup sugar

Cake:

1. Preheat oven to 350°F. Generously grease bottom and sides of a 9 by 13-inch metal baking pan. Set aside.

2. Separate egg yolks from whites, setting white aside (do not refrigerate). Cream sugar and butter together in the large bowl using an electric mixer at medium speed until yellow and fluffy. Add egg yolks and beat 2 to 3 minutes until light.

3. Using a medium bowl, sift flour and baking powder together.

4. In the second medium bowl, combine milk and vanilla.

5. Slowly add the milk/vanilla mixture to the butter/sugar mixture. Alternate with the flour/baking powder. Beat well each time. Batter should be smooth, but do not overbeat as cake can fall apart. This happened to me one time. It looked like an earthquake split the Tres Leches cake in two.

6. In the third medium bowl, beat egg white with cream of tartar until soft peaks form.

7. Fold egg whites into batter carefully using a large spatula.

8. Pour in greased cake pan. Bake for 25 to 30 minutes until golden. Allow to cool completely.

Tres Leches Cake – A Mystery

Nobody knows exactly where this sweet and insanely rich cake comes
from. Some say it originated in Mexico where it became the rage to serve
it at parties. Others claim it originated in Nicaragua. Well, Puerto Ricans
claim it originated on their island.

Since this cake is so popular in hot, Latin and Caribbean countries where
lots of tinned milk is used, I have concluded that the recipe must have
come on the back of a can of evaporated milk. If anyone has any further
information to add, please contact me at: Angelaspenceley1@msn.com

Three milks:

1. Whisk light cream, evaporated milk and sweetened condensed
   milk together.
2. Prick top of cooled cake with a fork or toothpick. Pour over top of
   cake and allow to soak while whipping cream for topping. Invert
   on cake plate.

Topping:

1. Whip heavy cream in a chilled medium bowl for 2 minutes.
   Gradually beat in sugar until stiff peaks form.
2. Generously ice top of cake with whipped topping. Serve at once.

Yield: 10 to 12 servings

Rum Chocolate Cake

*Rich and moist, this intensely chocolate-flavored cake is perfect for
beginning bakers as it is mixed right in the saucepan that melts the
chocolate.*

vegetable shortening to grease
two $8^{1}/_{2}$- by $4^{1}/_{2}$- by $2^{1}/_{2}$-
inch loaf pans
2 tablespoons unsweetened
cocoa powder
8 ounces unsweetened
chocolate
$^{3}/_{4}$ cup butter
1 cup strong coffee
$^{3}/_{4}$ cup dark rum, plus additional
$^{1}/_{2}$ cup to soak cake

2 eggs, plus 1 yolk
2 teaspoons vanilla extract
$^{1}/_{2}$ teaspoon almond extract
2 cups sifted cake flour
$1^{1}/_{2}$ cups sugar
1 teaspoon baking soda
$^{1}/_{4}$ teaspoon salt
$^{3}/_{4}$ cup semi-sweet chocolate
bits

1. Preheat oven to 275°. Grease the two loaf pans and dust with the 2 tablespoons cocoa powder. Using the cocoa powder instead of flour avoids a white-floured appearance to the chocolate cake.
2. Melt chocolate and butter in a heavy-bottomed 4-quart pan over low heat, stirring constantly. Whisk in coffee and $^3/_4$ cup rum, stirring until incorporated. Remove from heat and cool for 10 minutes.
3. Beat in eggs, vanilla and almond extract.
4. Sift flour, sugar, baking soda and salt together. Gradually beat in flour mixture to chocolate egg mixture using a wooden spoon or wire whisk for 4 to 5 minutes until smooth. Fold in chocolate bits.
5. Divide batter between two pans. Bake for 55 minutes or until a toothpick inserted in center comes out clean.
6. Remove from oven and lightly prick top of loaves with a fork. Drizzle remaining $^1/_2$ cup of rum equally over the still warm cakes. Allow to sit for 15 minutes in the pans.
7. Invert on greased rack, then flip over so that rum-soaked side faces up. Serve warm with whipped cream.

Yield: two 8$^1/_2$- by 4$^1/_2$- by 2$^1/_2$-inch loaves

Tip —Frosting A Cake

Frosting a cake successfully need not be daunting if you follow a few simple tips.

Cool cake first otherwise the frosting will liquefy from the cake's heat and run down the sides.

Crumbs in frosting: Freeze cakes for 20 minutes. Ice with a thin layer of frosting, return to freezer for 10 minutes, then finish frosting cake.

Smooth finish: Use your blowdryer over the tops and sides of cake like the pros do.

Avoiding a mess: Place narrow strips of waxed paper between the cake and the plate. Remove wax strips and discard after frosting.

Fresh Coconut Cake
(Bizcocho de Coco)

Light, tender and moist. Use freshly grated coconut meat for best flavor and texture. The addition of lemon to both the cake and the following frosting adds a lovely dimension to an otherwise typical coconut cake.

shortening to grease two 9-inch round cake pans
2 tablespoons flour
1 teaspoon fresh grated lemon rind
3/4 cup vegetable shortening
1 1/2 cups sugar
3 eggs, separated, plus 1 extra white, room temperature
2 1/4 cups cake flour
2 teaspoons baking powder
1/2 teaspoon baking soda
1/2 teaspoon salt
1/4 cup cream of coconut (the canned, sweetened kind used to make piña coladas)
3/4 cup milk
3 tablespoons fresh lemon juice
3 cups fresh grated coconut meat

1. Preheat oven to 375°F. Generously grease and flour (using the 2 tablespoons flour) the two cake pans.

2. Cream shortening in large bowl using a hand mixer set on medium for 1 minute until glossy. Beat in sugar until light and smooth. Beat in egg yolks one at a time, stirring in lemon rind.

3. Sift flour, baking powder, baking soda and salt together onto a piece of waxed paper.

4. Beat in one third of the flour mixture while mixer is still running. Alternate with cream of coconut, milk and lemon juice until all dry and wet ingredients are incorporated and smooth. Fold in grated coconut.

5. Rinse off beater blades and beat egg white (4) in a separate small bowl until stiff, glossy peaks form (but not dry).

6. Gently fold egg whites into cake batter 1/3 at a time.

7. Divide batter equally between two cake pans.

8. Bake for 25 to 30 minutes until a toothpick inserted in center comes out clean. Cool in pans for 10 minutes.

9. Gently invert on greased cake rack. Allow to cool completely before frosting with Fluffy Coconut Frosting.

Yield: 12 servings

Fluffy Coconut Frosting
(Azucarado Esponjoso de Coco)

1 1/2 cups sugar
1/4 teaspoon cream of tartar
1/4 teaspoon salt
3 egg whites
1/4 cup water

1 teaspoon fresh grated lemon
  rind
1 teaspoon vanilla extract
1/2 cup fresh grated coconut

1. Fill the bottom half of a double boiler with 1 1/2 inches of water. Bring to a simmer.

2. Combine sugar, cream of tartar, salt, egg whites and water in top of double boiler. Before placing over hot water, beat with a handheld mixer on low speed for 30 seconds until blended.

3. Place top of double boiler over water and beat continuously over low heat until frosting stands in peaks, about 5 to 7 minutes.

4. Remove from heat at once and continue to beat for 2 minutes until thick.

5. Fold in lemon rind, vanilla and grated coconut before frosting cake.

Yield: about 3 to 4 cups

'Gypsy's Arm' Sponge Roll
with Guava Filling
(Brazo Gitano con Guava)

My friend Anna's aunt, Doritza Romano, provided this recipe for the best sponge-cake jelly roll I ever had. The cornstarch gives it a firm, springy texture that won't break apart when rolled. The filling is clear with the delicate, perfumey taste of guava.

Sponge Roll:
5 eggs, separated
2 teaspoons vanilla extract
1/2 teaspoon lemon extract
1/2 teaspoon salt
1/2 cup granulated sugar
1/3 cup sifted cornstarch
1/3 cup sifted all-purpose flour
confectioner's sugar

Filling:
1 cup sugar
3 tablespoons cornstarch sifted
1/2 teaspoon salt
3/4 cup water
1/4 cup guava paste, chopped
1/2 cup fresh lemon juice

Sponge Roll:

1. Preheat oven to 357°. Grease a 10½ by 15½-inch jelly-roll pan and line with wax paper. Grease and flour the wax paper also.
2. Beat egg yolks with vanilla and lemon extract in a medium bowl. Set aside.
3. Beat egg whites until foamy. Add salt and keep beating until soft peaks form. Sprinkle in granulated sugar and beat until stiff, but not dry peaks form.
4. Scoop egg whites on top of egg yolks. Sift flour and cornstarch over top. Cut in gently with a rubber spatula until blended.
5. Spoon onto prepared pan. Bake for 10 to 12 minutes until a toothpick inserted in center comes out clean. Do not over bake, otherwise the cake will crack when rolling.
6. Dust a clean kitchen towel (non terry cloth) generously with confectioner's sugar.
7. Separate edges of cake from pan using a butter knife. Turn jelly roll out onto towel, removing the wax paper. Trim off any hard edges of cake.
8. Roll up cake lengthwise in the towel and allow to cool on a wire rack for 25 minutes.
9. Unroll carefully and spread with pastry cream or Guava Filling. Roll again without the towel, pressing lightly. Wrap in wax paper for 20 minutes, then unwrap and place on serving platter. Dust with confectioner's sugar. Slice with a bread knife.

Guava Filling:

1. Stir together the sugar, cornstarch, salt, water, guava paste and lemon juice. Bring to a boil.
2. Reduce heat and simmer for 1 minute, stirring constantly. Filling should thicken.
3. Remove from heat and chill in refrigerator until firm.
4. Follow instruction number 9 from above.

Yield: 14 to 16 slices

Hojaldre

Hojaldre keeps very well, if covered tightly, and actually improves in flavor as it ages.

3/4 cup butter
1 cup firmly packed brown
  sugar
4 large eggs
2 cups all-purpose flour
1 1/2 teaspoons baking powder
1 1/2 teaspoons cinnamon
1 1/2 teaspoons nutmeg

1/2 teaspoon ground cloves
1/4 teaspoon cardamom
1/4 teaspoon salt
1/3 cup whole milk
1/3 cup sweet red wine
confectioner's sugar, sifted (for
  garnishing)

1. Preheat oven to 350°F. Generously grease and flour a 9-inch by 3 1/2-inch tube pan.

2. Cream butter and sugar, beating until fluffy and nearly white. Whisk in eggs.

3. Sift together flour, baking powder, cinnamon, nutmeg, clove, cardamom and salt on wax paper. Repeat process twice more.

4. Add 1/4 quarter of the flour mixture at a time to the egg mixture, combining well. Repeat until all of flour is incorporated, alternating milk and wine. Batter should be smooth.

5. Pour batter into prepared pan and bake for 55 to 60 minutes until a toothpick inserted in center comes out clean.

6. Remove from oven and cool in pan on wire rack for 8 minutes. Invert cake on greased wire rack. Flip again so top is facing up and cool until room temperature, about 60 minutes.

7. Place on cake platter and dust with confectioner's sugar.

Yield: 8 to 10 servings

Basic Pie Crust

2 1/2 cups all-purpose flour, plus
  extra for dusting
3/4 teaspoon salt
1 tablespoon sugar
12 tablespoons unsalted butter,
  refrigerated, cut in small
  1/4 pieces

8 tablespoons vegetable
  shortening, refrigerated
6 tablespoons ice water

1. Combine flour, salt and sugar in food processor (use lower blade only, remove grating blade).
2. Add butter pieces and pulse until flour is pebbly. Add shortening by teaspoonfuls and continue to pulse 4 or 5 more times.
3. Scoop flour mixture into medium bowl. Sprinkle ice water over top. Using an up and down motion with a large spoon, combine until you can form a smooth ball. Add an extra tablespoon of water if needed.
4. Divide dough into two and press into shape of a flat ball. Dust with flour and refrigerate for 30 minutes.
5. Sprinkle a $1/4$ cup flour over work surface and rolling pin. Press down lightly on dough and roll back and forth. Rotate dough on surface and continue to roll out evenly, forming a circle. Diameter of dough should be 2 inches larger than pie plate.
6. Fold dough in half, than in half again. Place dough inside pie plate and unfold. Tuck pastry dough into corners of pie plate.
7. Trim dough down to $1/2$ inch overlap of pie plate. Tuck dough under, so that a $1/4$ inch lip remains. Press down lightly.

Yield: 2 unbaked pie crusts

Mango Pie (Pastel de Mango)

If by some chance you have leftover pie, freeze it as it keeps well.

1 recipe for Basic Pie Crust
$1/4$ cup granulated sugar
$1/2$ cup brown sugar
3 tablespoons tapioca
1 tablespoon lemon juice
1 teaspoon grated lemon zest
1 teaspoon fresh grated ginger root

$1/4$ teaspoon nutmeg
$1/4$ teaspoon cinnamon
$1/4$ teaspoon cardamom
$1/2$ teaspoon salt
6 cups peeled, pitted and sliced mango

1. Prepare Basic Pie Crust as directed.
2. Adjust oven rack to center position. Preheat oven to 400°F.
3. Roll one dough ball into a 12-inch disk. Fold dough in half, then in half again. Place in center of deep dish pie plate. Unfold and press dough into corners.
4. Combine sugars, tapioca, lemon juice, lemon zest, grated ginger, spices and salt in a large bowl. Add mango and toss gently to coat. Allow to sit for 10 minutes.

5. Scoop fruit into center of pie shell, pressing down gently, but leaving fruit slightly mounded in center.

6. Roll out second dough ball into 12-inch disk. Place over filling.

7. Trim top within $1/2$ inch of edge and tuck underneath. Press down with tines of fork to seal.

8. Bake until golden, about 25 minutes. Reduce heat to 350°F and bake additional 25 minutes.

9. Remove from oven and place on wire rack to cool, about 2 hours. Serve at once.

Yield: 8 servings

Shortbread Cookies (Mantecaditos)

Sandy and crumbly as perfect shortbread shoud be.

$1/2$ pound butter, room temperature
$1^1/2$ teaspoons almond extract
$1/2$ cup confectioner's sugar

2 tablespoons granulated sugar
2 cups all-purpose flour
$1/4$ teaspoon salt

1. Preheat oven to 350°F.

2. Cream butter with almond extract in a medium bowl, gradually whipping in sugars until and fluffy.

3. Sift flour and salt onto a wax paper. Gradually fold into butter mixture until well-combined.

4. Flour a rolling pin and roll out the dough until $1/4$ inch thick. Cut into rectangles, squares or use a cookie cutter.

5. Place on ungreased cookie sheets. Prick each cookie with a fork and bake for 20 minutes or until golden on the edges.

6. Slide off cookie sheet immediately and cool on wire rack.

Yield: 24, 1 x 2 inch cookies

Taste of Puerto Rico

Almond Cookies (Polvorones)

These cookies resemble Viennese Crescents and the generous use of butter makes them melt in your mouth.

1/2 pound butter, room
  temperature
1 egg yolk
1 teaspoon almond extract

3/4 confectioner's sugar, plus
  extra dusting cookies
2 cups flour
1 cup ground almonds

1. Preheat oven to 300°F.
2. Cream butter in a medium bowl with a hand whisk until shiny. Whisk in egg and almond extract. Gradually beat in sugar, beating until light and fluffy.
3. Whisk in flour and ground almonds, combining thoroughly.
4. Shape into 2-inch crescents with your fingers. Roll in confectioner's sugar and bake on ungreased cookie sheets for 12 to 15 minutes, until lightly browned.
5. Slide off cookie sheets at once and cool on wire racks. Dust again with confectioner's sugar before serving.

Yield: 36 to 48 cookies

Coconut Crunch (Turroncitos de Coco)

One finds this candy all over Puerto Rico, even at the 24-hour gas stations!

2 cups coconut milk
3 cups sugar
1/2 teaspoon almond extract

1/2 teaspoon vanilla
1/8 teaspoon mace

1. Boil coconut milk, sugar, almond extract, vanilla and mace in a deep kettle or pot. Reduce heat to medium and cook without stirring until syrup thickens into hard ball stage (258°F, candy thermometer).
2. Grease a marble slab and pour candy mixture over it to allow cooling.
3. When beginning to firm, but not harden, pull as for taffy. Pull out, bring back, then pull out again. Keep going until candy whitens.
4. Without wasting a moment, roll candy into long logs, about 1 1/2 inches thick. Slice into 2 inch pieces. Best if wrapped in wax paper.

Yield: about 48 pieces

Coconut Caramels
(Dulce de Leche con Coco)

Once you eat caramel with coconut, you'll never go back to plain caramel candy again.

1 cup grated coconut
1 cup evaporated milk
1 cup sweetened condensed milk
1/2 cup packed brown sugar
1/2 teaspoon salt
3/4 cup Crisco™
1 teaspoon almond extract
1/2 teaspoon rose extract

1. Soak coconut in evaporated milk for 1 hour. Place in medium sauce pan along with sweetened condensed milk, brown sugar, salt and 1/3 of the Crisco™. Stir in almond and rose extract.
2. Cook over moderate heat until mixture forms a soft ball in cold water, 235°F on candy thermometer.
3. Stir in remaining Crisco™ and cook until mixture reaches 250°F.
4. Scoop candy into buttered or Criscoed™ shallow glass baking dish.
5. Slice into 1-inch squares when cool. Wrap each caramel in wax candy.

Yield: approximately 100 pieces

Mango Ice Cream
(Mantecado de Mango)

This remind me of childhood vacations in New Hampshire and peach vanilla ice cream bought at the country store.

4 large ripe mangoes, peeled, and diced
3 eggs, lightly beaten
1 1/2 cups sugar
2 cups half and half
1 cup whipping cream
1/2 teaspoon salt
1 tablespoon fresh lime juice
2 tablespoons vanilla

1. Puree mango in food processor. Refrigerate. Combine eggs, sugar, half and half, whipping cream and salt in a heavy saucepan over moderate heat, stirring constantly until mixture nearly boils. Keep from boiling.
3. Remove from heat and stir in lime juice and vanilla. Allow to cool to room temperature, about 45 minutes, stirring occasionally.
4. Fold in chilled mango puree. Pour into ice cream freezer and follow manufacturer's instructions.

Yield: nearly 2 quarts

Taste of Puerto Rico

Banana Ice Cream
(Mantecado de Plátano)

This is my favorite ice cream in the world. Well, next to Chocolate Rum Ice Cream…

³/4 cup sugar
3 large eggs, beaten
2 teaspoons cornstarch, sifted
1 teaspoon vanilla extract
¹/4 teaspoon salt

1 cup half and half
1 cup heavy whipping cream
4 large ripe bananas
¹/4 cup banana liqueur

1. Combine sugar and eggs in a small bowl until creamy. Slowly add cornstarch, vanilla extract and salt, combining well. Set aside.
2. Heat half and half and heavy cream in a medium saucepan over moderate heat, bringing to a boil while stirring constantly.
3. Reduce heat and whisk in egg mixture. Stir constantly until mixture thickens. Remove from heat.
4. Pour through a strainer into a bowl.
5. Mash bananas in separate bowl and fold into custard mixture. Allow to cool to room temperature.
6. Stir in banana liqueur and pour into ice cream freezer. Follow manufacturer's instructions.

Yield: almost 2 quarts

Chocolate Rum Ice Cream
(Mantecado de Chocolate y Ron)

Chocolate and rum—a heady combination.

1¹/4 cups sugar
¹/4 teaspoon salt
2 teaspoons cornstarch, sifted
4 large egg yolks, lightly beaten
3 cups half and half
1 cup heavy whipping cream

3 ounces good quality baking chocolate, melted in top of double boiler
¹/2 teaspoon almond extract
1 teaspoon vanilla extract
¹/4 cup Puerto Rican rum

1. Sift together the sugar, salt and cornstarch in a small bowl. Stir in beaten eggs until creamy. Set aside.

2. Heat half and half and cream in a large saucepan over medium heat, stirring constantly until very hot, 7 to 8 minutes, but not boiling.

3. Gradually stir in sugar mixture, stirring constantly until mixture thickens.

4. Remove from heat and stir in melted chocolate. Allow to cool for 15 minutes then stir in almond and vanilla extract.

5. Cool to room temperature, stirring occasionally. Stir in rum.

6. Pour into ice cream freezer and follow manufacturer's instructions.

Yield: over 1 quart

Coconut Sherbert (Helado de Coco)

Lovely, for those who wish to avoid dairy.

2 cups fresh coconut milk
1 teaspoon grated lemon rind
$^1/_2$ teaspoon almond extract

$^1/_2$ teaspoon salt
2$^1/_2$ cups sugar

1. Combine coconut milk, lemon rind, almond extract and salt in medium saucepan over moderate heat.

2. Stir in sugar until dissolved. Remove from heat and allow to cool.

3. Pour mixture into ice cream maker and follow manufacturer's directions.

4. Pour into freezedr-proof container and freeze for 4 hours before serving.

Yield: 4 servings

Chapter Eleven

Rum Drinks

All of the drinks in this chapter naturally feature Puerto Rican rum. Other rums may be substituted, with almost as pleasing a result. As always, do not drink and drive or operate heavy equipment while under the influence of alcohol. Caution applies to pregnant women, those with heart conditions or other health issues.

For a comprehensive source for tropical and Caribbean drink recipes, using vodka, gin, rum, tequila, as well as rum and exotic liqueurs, please see Don't Drink The Water!, a nearly 300-page book filled with drinks which includes an appetizer chapter.

This is the impatiens, a flower found in the rainforest, and usually around the coqui frog.

Bacardi Cocktail

2 ounces light Bacardi Rum
1 ounce sour mix

splash of Grenadine syrup

1. Fill a shaker with ice, rum, sour mix and Grenadine. Strain into a chilled rocks glass.

Yield: 1 drink

Bacardi Mama

1½ ounces light rum
½ ounce Triple Sec
1 ounce orange juice

1 ounce pineapple juice
splash of Grenadine syrup

1. Fill a tall glass with ice. Add rum, Triple Sec, orange and pineapple juice and Grenadine. Stir.

Yield: 1 drink

Banana Daiquiri

No good drink book is complete without a recipe for Banana Daiquiri.

2 ounces light or gold rum
½ ounce Banana liqueur
2 ounces light cream

1 small ripe banana
½ cup crushed ice

1. Whirl all ingredients in blender until frothy. Pour into a tall glass.

Yield: 1 drink

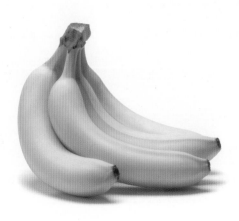

Taste of Puerto Rico

Christmas Rum and Coconut Punch (Coquito)

Coconut eggnog, a traditional Puerto Rican holiday drink, is the quintessential tropical eggnog. Commercially canned coconut may be substituted successfully.

2 cups fresh coconut milk
$1/4$ cup sugar
$1/4$ teaspoon salt
$1/4$ teaspoon cinnamon
1 egg yolk

2 cups white Puerto Rican rum, or to taste
$1/4$ cup fresh grated coconut
ground nutmeg

1. Put $1/2$ cup of coconut milk, sugar, salt and cinnamon in a blender. Whirl until sugar is dissolved.
2. Add remaining coconut milk, egg yolk and cinnamon and process until smooth.
3. Add rum gradually and puree 2 minutes until frothy.
4. Pour into clean bottles and refrigerate. Serve in liqueur glasses, dust with nutmeg.

Yield: a little over 4 cups

Health Tip—Raw Eggs

To avoid salmonella contamination, use an egg substitute. These can be found in the refrigerator and frozen area of your grocery store. Usually they contain pasteurized eggs whites, vegetable oil, food coloring and vitamins. As a bonus, many substitutes contain no cholesterol and are low in fat.

Mojito

1 1/2 ounces lime juice
1 teaspoon powdered sugar
3 mint leaves

2 ounces light rum
crushed ice
club soda

1. Combine sugar and lime juice in a highball glass. Add mint leaves and crush against sides of glass with a spoon. Add crushed ice and rum. Stir. Float club soda to top of glass.

Yield: 1 drink

Piña Colada

When actress Joan Collins sipped her first piña colada at the former Beachcomber's Bar in the Caribe Hilton, she asserted it was better than slapping Betty Davis in the face. The creator of this famous drink was Ramon "Monchito" Marrerro in 1954. This recipe can easily be doubled.

2 ounces light rum
splash of 151 proof rum
   (optional)
1 ounce light cream

1 ounce coconut cream
4 ounces pineapple juice
1/2 cup crushed ice

1. Whirl all ingredients in blender until frothy.

Yield: 1 drink

Planter's Punch

Another recipe no self-respecting drink guide would be without.

2 ounces dark rum
1 ounce fresh lime juice

1 teaspoon Grenadine syrup
dash of angostura bitters

1. Shake all ingredients in a cocktail shaker filled with ice. Strain into a tall glass, Garnish with a sprig of mint, cherry and an orange.

Yield: 1 drink

Puerto Rican Sangria
(Sangria Criolla)

Watch out for this sangria. The rum sneaks up on you.

1 cup fresh pineapple, cut in
   1-inch cubes
3/4 cup white rum
2 cups red wine
2 cups lemon-lime soda
1 cup pineapple juice

1/2 cup fresh lime juice
1 cup frozen passionfruit pulp,
   thawed
1/4 cup frozen orange juice
   concentrate, thawed

1. Soak the pineapple cubes in the rum overnight. Two days is better. The rum will smell heavenly.
2. Pour the rum and pineapple bits into a large glass or ceramic pitcher. Do not use plastic as it will add an unappealing off taste.
3. Add wine, soda, pineapple, lime, passionfruit and orange juice to pitcher. Stir.
4. Chill at least 3 hours.

Yield: over 2 quarts

Rum Punch

2 ounces light rum
1 ounce orange juice
1 ounce pineapple juice
1 ounce cranberry juice

1/2 ounce lemon or lime juice
splash of Grenadine syrup
club soda

1. Fill a tall glass with ice. Add all other ingredients, except club soda. Fill remainder of glass with club soda. Stir. Garnish with thin lemon slices.

Yield: 1 drink

Zombie

For those of you who have read my other cookbooks, you'll know I put a version of the ubiquitous Zombie in nearly all my books. This was probably the first alcoholic drink I ever had. I was 18 years old, at the Mad Hatter on the island of Nantucket. It literally put me under the table.

1 ounce light rum
1 ounce dark rum
1 ounce cherry brandy
1 ounce orange juice

1 ounce pineapple juice
1 ounce lime juice
1 cup crushed ice

1. Whirl all ingredients in blender until smooth. Divide equally between two tall glasses.

Yield: 2 drinks

Lovebird amidst tropical foliage

Bibliography

David Joachim with Andrew Schloss, Jan Newberry, Maryellen Driscoll, Paul E. Piccuito, *Brilliant Food Tips and Cooking Tricks,* United States, Rodale Publishing 2001, 604 pages.

Harry S. Pariser, *Adventure Guide to Puerto Rico*, 3rd Edition, New Jersey, Hunter Publishing, 1996, 329 pages.

Québec/Amérique International. *The Visual Food Encylopedia,* Montreal, Québec, Les Éditions Québec/Amérique Inc. 1996, 695 pages.

Wiley Publishing, *Frommer's Puerto Rico,* 6th Edition, New York, NY, Wiley Publishing Inc. 2002, 278 pages.

Index

Order Cookbooks now in time for the holidays!

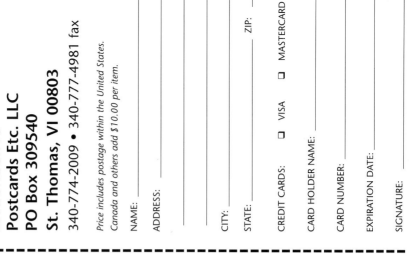

Send the gift of a Caribbean memory
prices include postage within the continental U.S.

ITEM	QUANTITY	PRICE EACH	TOTAL
Virgin Island & Caribbean Cookbooks			
A Taste of the British Virgin Islands, *approx. 60 pages*		$14.95	
A Taste of the Virgin Islands, Too *approx. 48 pages, color photos*		$13.95	
A Taste of St. John, *83 pages*		$14.95	
A Taste of St. Croix, *approx. 60 pages*		$12.95	
A Taste of the Caribbean, *approx. 300 pages*		$24.95	
Just Add Rum! Food & Drink cookbook, *approx. 120 pages*		$14.95	
A Taste of Puerto Rico, Too, *approx. 400 pages*		$24.95	
A Taste of Puerto Rico, *118 color pages*		$16.95	
Guidebooks			
U.S. Virgin Island Guidebook, *96 color pages*		$24.95	
British Virgin Island Guidebook, *96 color pages*		$24.95	
Puerto Rico Guidebook, Spanish or English *(specify), 96 color pages*		$19.95	
St. Martin Guidebook, *64 color pages*		$14.95	
Kids Coloring & Sticker Books			
Pirate or Virgin Island *(specify)*		$ 9.95	

MAIL CHECK TO:

Postcards Etc. LLC
PO Box 309540
St. Thomas, VI 00803
340-774-2009 • 340-777-4981 fax

Price includes postage within the United States.
Canada and others add $10.00 per item.

NAME: _____

ADDRESS: _____

_____

CITY: _____

STATE: _____ ZIP: _____

CREDIT CARDS: ☐ VISA ☐ MASTERCARD

CARD HOLDER NAME: _____

CARD NUMBER: _____

EXPIRATION DATE: _____

SIGNATURE: _____